DAMSEL, Arise!

JENNIFER SCHWIRZER

DAMSEL, Arise!

Pacific Press®
Publishing Association

Nampa, Idaho | Oshawa, Ontario, Canada
www.pacificpress.com

Cover design by Gerald Lee Monks
Cover design resources from iStockphoto.com | HstrongART
Inside design by Kristin Hansen-Mellish

Unless otherwise noted, all Scripture quotations are from the New King James
Version®. Copyright © 1982 by Thomas Nelson. Used by permission. All rights
reserved.

Scripture quotations marked KJV are from the King James Version.

Scripture quotations marked NIV® are from THE HOLY BIBLE, NEW INTER-
NATIONAL VERSION®. Copyright © 1973, 1978, 1984, 2011 by Biblica, Inc.®
Used by permission. All rights reserved worldwide.

Scripture quotations marked NLT are taken from the Holy Bible, New Living
Translation, copyright © 1996, 2004, 2007, 2013, 2015 by Tyndale House
Foundation. Used by permission of Tyndale House Publishers, Inc., Carol Stream,
Illinois 60188. All rights reserved.

The author assumes full responsibility for the accuracy of all facts and quotations
as cited in this book.

Additional copies of this book are available by calling toll-free 1-800-765-6955 or
by visiting http://www.adventistbookcenter.com.

Library of Congress Cataloging-in-Publication Data
Names: Schwirzer, Jennifer Jill, 1957- author.
Title: Damsel, Arise! / Jennifer Schwirzer.
Description: Nampa : Pacific Press Publishing Association, 2018.
Identifiers: LCCN 2018000400 | ISBN 978-0-8163-6371-1 (pbk. : alk. paper)
Subjects: LCSH: Jesus Christ—Relations with women. | Women in the Bible.
Classification: LCC BT590.W6 S39 2018 | DDC 248.8/43—dc23 LC record
available at https://lccn.loc.gov/2018000400

March 2018

Dedication

Dedicated to the thousands of women I have tried to help during the last thirty years. I place you in the hands of Jesus, who bids you rise to your fullest potential.

Contents

Introduction

I grew up in a conventional American home. As a young woman, I found myself in the midst of full-swing, second-wave feminism with its message of workplace equality and women's rights. Embracing it passionately, I surrounded myself with like-minded women, finally landing in a college environment saturated with militant feminist professors, among other things.

Somehow, in that first year of college, God broke through to me, and I surrendered my life to Jesus Christ. As I tried to explain my newfound faith to fellow students, I lost friend after friend until in desperation for Christian fellowship I joined a Seventh-day Adventist community a short distance from the university. This group deeply appreciated the writings of Ellen G. White, who was a woman believed by Adventists to be endowed with the gift of prophecy. In Mrs. White, I saw a woman of extraordinary drive and ambition and a woman God used to lead millions through the words she wrote during her lifetime. I knew that many churches believed the Bible opposed everything about feminism;

but in Ellen G. White and Seventh-day Adventism, I saw a more nuanced approach that accepted some aspects while rejecting others. In both her example and her writings, this woman, who had been forced to drop out of school in the third grade because of an accident, helped me to understand how deeply God believes in women.

Though my concepts were formed early in my Christian experience, they needed to be tested. As a young mother of two, I sensed God calling me into a part-time Bible teaching and writing ministry. I had wanted to be a singer, but health problems compromised my voice too much to make that plan practical. God impressed upon me one day that I had always been a "good talker" and writer. He seemed to be saying, *Why don't you develop those gifts?*

"But God!" I said, "In my church, the women don't speak and write, really. I mean, they write cookbooks and children's books and stories but not theological books. Not very often, anyway."

Maybe I want you to help change that.

So I began. Little did I realize the obstacles and prejudices I would face. I once asked the director of an evangelism ministry, "Why don't you hire a woman evangelist?"

"None of the churches would want a woman," came the reply.

Later, as I was reading a magazine published by that ministry, I noticed how the leader said that while women weren't permitted to be pastors, they could be evangelists. *Great*, I thought. But then I turned the page and their entire roster of evangelists stared back at me. Not one female evangelist.

Wait, I thought. *If we all agree that the Bible accepts female evangelists, then why don't we have any?*

I set out to create an apologetic of sorts for more inclusion of women in spiritual ministry. My church has long wrestled with whether or not to ordain women as pastors. For the most part, I ignored the politics, preferring to address what I considered the underlying issues that, if not corrected, would just lead to infinite forms of imbalance. I developed the seminar Damsel, Arise: What's Killing Women and How Jesus Raises Us Back to Life to address not only the external assaults on our potential as women, but our own self-sabotaging of that potential. I presented that seminar countless times before I realized it needed a printed form. Each chapter in this book includes a question to consider and respond to in the space provided.

With militant feminism in one ditch and unbiblical male dominance in the other, I began to try to walk behind Jesus on the narrow way. Those beautiful feet of Jesus; feet that had been nailed to a cross for me—but only after they had been anointed with costly perfume by a woman—feet that brought the good news of my potential as a human being and of God's belief in me, even when no one else saw the possibilities; those beautiful feet carved out a path for me to follow. The results of that journey you find here in *Damsel, Arise!*

Chapter 1

In His Image — Male and Female

Discovering God's Perfect Plan in the Beginning

On that first morning, sweeter than a tree-ripened peach, more fragrant than a flowering valley, God felt a void. In the midst of the verdure; the teeming animal life; the crystal, rushing water, something was missing. That something was us.*

"So God created man in His own image; in the image of God He created him; male and female He created them" (Genesis 1:27).

God wanted more than beauty and perfection and more than artistic satisfaction. He longed for face time with beings He could understand and who could understand Him.

He craved our presence before He made us.

Allow this single fact to sink down into your soul: You are meant to be. Let this truth refute any doubts of your

---

* This chapter originally appeared in Jennifer Jill Schwirzer, "Male and Female—in His Image," *Sabbath School Net* (blog), May 11, 2015, http://ssnet.org/blog/male-female-in-his-image/.

value. Step back from the pressures of your family, your society, and your church—pressures that sometimes reduce your value to your appearance, your performance, or your achievements—and let God whisper to you the message of Eden. "I made you in My image. I needed someone like Me. You are the outflowing of an exquisite plan that was put in place from the beginning of time. I have great dreams for you; but even before you fulfill them, I value you just for being a human, made to love like Me."

With that awareness in place, let us walk through the crowning act of the Genesis story—the creation of man and woman—and witness God's artistry.

"And the LORD God formed man of the dust of the ground, and breathed into his nostrils the breath of life; and man became a living being" (Genesis 2:7). God bent down to the loose dirt and sculpted a man; the Hebrew word *yatsar*, which is translated as "formed" in English, refers to squeezing something into shape, as a potter would. God shaped a noble head; a broad chest; powerful arms; washboard abs; firm, strong legs and feet; all squared off and angled in that way of men—he was gorgeous. Then performing something like CPR (cardiopulmonary resuscitation), God breathed into the man, and his inanimate form hummed into life.

> The LORD God planted a garden eastward in Eden, and there He put the man whom He had formed. And out of the ground the LORD God made every tree grow that is pleasant to the sight and good for food. The tree of life was also in the midst of the garden, and the tree of the knowledge of good and evil.
>
> Now a river went out of Eden to water the garden,

and from there it parted and became four riverheads (verses 8–10).

God made a Garden for Adam and placed him in its midst. The ground pumped out fruit-laden trees, which were watered by a coursing river that branched out into four heads, forming new rivers that swirled by lands enriched with clusters of gold and precious stones. The air pulsated with layers of contrapuntal birdsongs that weaved in and out of each other, while gentle winds swept through dancing, silvery grass.

"Dress and keep this garden," God instructed His new man-child, who must have gasped with joy. All was beauty and delight. The cosmic King and His steward of earth walked, talked, and laughed together during those first hours in Eden.

But something was still missing. That something was again us, but this time I mean women.

God could have stopped the creation process with Adam. After all, Adam was amazing! But he wasn't amazing enough. To fulfill His plan to reveal His love, God needed more. He needed the second half of the human race—woman. "It is not good that man should be alone," God said. "I will make him a helper comparable to him" (verse 18).

Designed with unalterable bonding features, we humans suffer when in isolation and we thrive when we are in relationships. In particular, married men have better health, fewer addictions, and longer lives. God knew Eve would raise the quality of Adam's life by leaps and bounds.

What does being a "helper" mean? *Ezer*, the Hebrew word for "helper," evokes images of someone surrounding and protecting another. *Ezer* lies about as far linguistically from *doormat* as one can get. An *ezer* is really a kind of hero. God planned to make Adam a heroine counterpart. Together, they would be quite the power couple.

"And the LORD God caused a deep sleep to fall on Adam, and he slept; and He took one of his ribs, and closed up the flesh in its place. Then the rib which the LORD God had taken from man He made into a woman" (verses 21, 22). He took a rib; He made a woman. The rib provided the raw material, and God's own hand powered and guided the process of making the woman. The original word for "made," *banah*, contrasts with Adam's *yatsar*. Did you get that? The Bible uses different verbs to describe the creation of Adam and of Eve! *Banah* alludes to building, as in constructing a house. (The English word *architecture* applies here.) *Yatsar* means something like "sculpted." God *sculpted* Adam but *built* Eve. Different formation processes mean different outcomes. God made us differently, and we turned out differently— by design.

The reason for this distinction emerges when we sink our hearts into the fact that we were made, male and female, in God's image, or *tselem*. *Tselem* means "represent." Here is a paraphrase of Genesis 1:27, "God created people to represent Him; to represent Him, God created people; male and female were made."

Let us break this down into a simple equation: Male + female = a representation of God. Our differences blend to form a picture of God.

If two things together create a representation, subtracting one results in a misrepresentation. Think of the color purple, which is a combination of blue and red. Pretend you have just been healed of blindness, and you see purple for the first time in your life. If I showed you blue, would that be sufficient to represent purple? No. How about red? No. Neither red nor blue would give you an adequate idea of the character of purple.

In the same way, neither male nor female alone give an adequate idea of the character of God. The electricity, the synergy, and the mystical (and sometimes mystifying) blending of the genders in marriage and in the church reveals God's character of love. Richard Davidson points out that in the original language of Genesis the creation of man and the creation of woman have the same number of words. Through this, he says, "The narrator underscores their equal importance."[1]

Woman and man have equal importance. I like the sound of that. How about you? Do most women want to be *more* important than men? I don't. But *less* important? I don't want that either.

Sinless and unselfish, Adam and Eve needed no hierarchy. Their relationship was an example of utter equality. Author Ellen White comments, "She was not to control him as the head, nor to be trampled under his feet as an inferior, but to stand by his side as an equal, to be loved and protected by him."[2] Peter Lombard echoes, "Eve was not taken from the feet of Adam to be his slave, nor from his head to be his lord, but from his side to be his beloved partner."[3]

It is true that Adam served as the head of the human race, even in that unfallen state. Being the firstborn of all creation, he stood as humanity's representative. Yet his headship didn't equate to being the "boss" of Eve. Because they had no taint of selfishness, Adam and Eve moved together like a well-choreographed dance. There were no missteps, no tension, just fluid, flawless harmony. But even as equals, individuality needed protection.

"Then the rib which the Lord God had taken from man He made into a woman, and He brought her to the man" (verse 22). The Bible clearly says that God "brought" the woman to Adam. In this simple statement, we see a fact implied: Eve connected with God *before* connecting with Adam. This speaks loudly to the need to put God first in our love lives. Women so often get lost in their relationships, especially the romantic ones. We so often sacrifice that which should never be sacrificed—our integrity and God-given selfhood—to hang on to a man. This tendency, apart from the sacred boundary of a God-centered marriage, proves ruinous to women.

Yet individuality and intimacy form a tension that must be balanced, lest both be lost. When we lose individuality, we lose intimacy because a healthy adult bond requires two mature *individuals*. The secret of preserving individuality lies in staying connected to God, the Creator of our individuality. God knew this, so He set aside face time with Eve. Moreover, He wants that same face time with you, for He claims the first and best of your affections.

Imagine Eve. Beautiful beyond words, shapely, bathed in light, her shining hair framing a feminine face, Eve turns her newly created eyes to her Maker and adores Him. Eye to eye, face to face, they commune as deep waves of affection wash between them like an ebbing tide. Then after unmeasured moments, He whispers, "There is someone I want you to meet."

So, for the first time, the two halves of a whole join

together. With their breaths catching in their throats and their hearts fluttering, they inspect each other's different-but-similar bodies. *Eyes, nose, mouth, arms, legs, but what is this? You are soft here, and I am firm. You are round where I am straight.* Awe and comfort mingle. They fit each other in ways they will discover throughout their lives.

And God rejoices. His plan bursts into life, like springtime.

Journaling

God spent time with Eve before bringing her to Adam. What does this tell you about God, yourself, and your relationships?

_____

_____

_____

_____

_____

_____

_____

_____

_____

_____

_____

_____

Damsel, Arise!

Prayer

Dear kind Creator,

How sweet to know that my existence came forth from Your deep desire for creatures made in Your image. At times, I have failed to see my value, God, and the beauty of Your design and plan in creating male and female. Enrich my understanding of Your creation. Fill my heart with a sense of purpose such that I will live each day in view of eternity. Amen.

---

1. Richard Davidson, "Headship, Submission, and Equality in Scripture," in *Women in Ministry: Biblical and Historical Perspectives*, ed. Nancy J. Vyhmeister (Berrien Springs, MI: Andrews University Press, 1998), 261.

2. Ellen G. White, *Patriarchs and Prophets* (Mountain View, CA: Pacific Press®, 1958), 46.

3. Peter Lombard, *The Book of Sentences* (ca. 1150), quoted in Paul Jewett, *Man as Male and Female* (Grand Rapids, MI: Eerdmans, 1975), 120.

Chapter 2

War Babies

How the War in Heaven Led to Our Creation

My husband and I never watch movies together, partly because we can't agree on which one to watch. Generally, men enjoy war stories and women love interpersonal dramas. In fact, research on gender and film preferences shows that men choose action movies three times more often than women and women choose romances eleven times more often than do their male counterparts.[1]

The story of planet Earth is a war story *and* a romance—a war between good and evil and a romance between God and the human race. It's called the great controversy, but it could also be called the great love story. It's a perfect story for men and women to watch together.

The impending threat

Little did Adam and Eve know, as they enjoyed their Eden paradise, that a certain tragedy loomed around them. These innocent ones had been born into a war. Their eyes must have grown wide as the angels explained to them the events that had led to their creation. Maybe they heard something like this:

God and His Son collaborated in creating you. They longed to display Their love and goodness, and They chose to do it through you. You were meant to be God's special ambassadors! All through this creative process, a certain "Lucifer, son of the morning," held very high privileges in heaven's courts (Isaiah 14:12). He was beautiful, brilliant, and talented, and was blessed by God with unique gifts and a specific calling. He was "the anointed cherub who covers . . . on the holy mountain of God." He "walked back and forth in the midst of fiery stones." He was "perfect in . . . [his] ways from the day . . . [he was] created" (Ezekiel 28:14, 15).

As if his beauty and brilliance weren't enough, he played "timbrels and pipes" (verse 13). The music— what glorious songs flowed from him! He sang harmony with himself, directing angel choirs with one hand and playing the timbrel with the other. The angels adored him.

But one day his spirit became troubled. His brows furrowed, and his eyes shifted to and fro. He began to murmur about God's law being oppressive and even insinuated that God Himself was on some kind of power trip. He implied that when the Father and the Son had cocreated the world, he should have been included in the decision. Approaching one angel after another, he tried to sell them on the idea that God's government was unfair and that he would make a better god.

A drawn-out struggle began. God said,

> "How you are fallen from heaven,
> O Lucifer, son of the morning!
> How you are cut down to the ground,
> You who weakened the nations!
> For you have said in your heart:
> 'I will ascend into heaven,
> I will exalt my throne above the stars of God;
> I will also sit on the mount of the congregation
> On the farthest sides of the north;
> I will ascend above the heights of the clouds,
> I will be like the Most High.'
> Yet you shall be brought down to Sheol,
> To the lowest depths of the Pit" (Isaiah 14:12–15).

But then as the conflict wore on, we saw God reach out to Lucifer tenderly, only to be rebuffed and misrepresented. Every interaction broke down into confusion and frustrated intentions. We stayed true to God, and we hoped that Lucifer would come to his senses and see that God's law, far from being an arbitrary imposition for power's sake, really served to protect the happiness and well-being of all His creatures. In fact, the law simply reflected God's heart of unselfish love.

But Lucifer kept seeing God, His law, and His government through a dark, dismal lens. About a third of our ranks gradually joined him, and we watched while he brainwashed them into believing they could never turn back. Finally, God did let go and cast Lucifer and his followers down to earth, saying,

> "Your pomp is brought down to Sheol,
> And the sound of your stringed instruments;
> The maggot is spread under you,
> And worms cover you" (verse 11).

Lucifer's prideful ascent ultimately sent him tumbling down to the depths of debasement. He became the devil and Satan. But even after his exile, God allowed him to live. God said that to destroy him then would have robbed us of an opportunity to see his true character. Our affection for him made it difficult for us to see his desperate narcissism.

Rather than obliterate the devil and his dissenters and demand unquestioning obedience from the loyal angels, God reinforced His purpose to reveal His true self by creating a race that would be so much like Him that He could say, "Look at them, and you will see Me." You are that special race, Adam and Eve. You are made in the image of God to show God to the universe. You "have been made a spectacle to the world, both to angels and to men" (1 Corinthians 4:9).

This beautiful Garden all around you and the animals that eat from your hand God has placed under natural law; they are governed fully by it and are unable to escape it. Only you, the first created human beings, have been made subject to moral law and been given a free will to choose obedience or disobedience. God took this death-defying risk because true love, obedience, and worship cannot exist in the absence of true freedom.

To provide an opportunity for your response to this

freely given love, God has placed one small test before you, Adam and Eve. The test is that tree over there—the tree of the knowledge of good and evil. You may not eat from that tree. Obey that simple command for a short testing period, and you will have proven yourselves safe. You will then fill the vacancies left by the fallen angels, and the wounds left by Lucifer's fall will heal at last.

Can you imagine the expressions on the faces of the man and the woman as they heard the odyssey that led to their existence? I am sure a mixture of emotions rose up in their hearts—awe, wonder, excitement, and ambition mingled with a few ripples of fear. God had planted a two-member church in Eden and called them to preach the good news of His unfathomable love to the entire cosmos.

Centuries later, Paul would say, "God's purpose in all this was to use the church to display his wisdom in its rich variety to all the unseen rulers and authorities in the heavenly places" (Ephesians 3:10, NLT). Through the church, which is comprised of people, God displays His wisdom to the rulers and authorities in heaven—the angels.

Let's boil that down further: God speaks through people to angels.

And how does He speak?

He speaks through men and women, who are made in His image. We halves of a whole must join together to fulfill the purpose for our creation. Marriage provides an excellent opportunity for this joining. But it is not the only opportunity; and for some, it is not an option at all.

Where can the children, single adults, widows and widowers, and all others not called into marriage still fulfill their purpose of synergistic, male-and-female blending and join together to share the love of God and portray His image to the universe? The church, of course, which is the community of God followers, first established in Eden, ever growing and continuing to this day.

And what are the specific differences that make this synergy so powerful? Dare we talk about them? Dare we not?

Journaling

When the angels observe your life, what do they see? What do you want them to see?

_____

_____

_____

_____

_____

_____

_____

_____

_____

_____

_____

Prayer

Beloved, embattled King,

I can't begin to feel the distress Your heart has carried for thousands of years over the effects of sin upon Your creation. Through love and fellowship with others, use me to silence the lies of the enemy and shine forth Your image. Amen.

---

1. Olivia Chausson, "Who Watches What? Assessing the Impact of Gender and Personality on Film Preferences," MyPersonality Project, last modified November 18, 2010, http://mypersonality.org/wiki/doku.php?id=movie_tastes_and _personality.

Chapter 3

Different but Equal

*Male and Female Differences
and How They Work Together*

A story is told of an English professor who wrote the sentence "Woman without her man is nothing" on a blackboard and directed his students to punctuate it correctly.

The men wrote, "Woman, without her man, is nothing."

The women wrote, "Woman: without her, man is nothing."

They were both wrong. And they were both right. Without each other, we are nothing in terms of fulfilling our purpose of reflecting the image of God.

What did God have in mind in creating Adam and Eve? Could He not have made a single-sex race? Why the binary nature of humans?[1] Beyond the obvious physical differences, men and women differ in countless intellectual and emotional ways. These are elusive and difficult to quantify, but contemplating them helps us to grasp how the blend of male and female creates a divinely inspired synergy that reveals deep mysteries about the love of God.

A word of caution about male-female differences: While we observe these generalities, we should avoid stereotypes. The male versus female traits spread over a bell curve, with overlap at the extremes. For instance, most men are taller than most women, but startling exceptions exist. Such was the case back in the seventeenth century when a woman named Trijntje Cornelisdochter Keever grew to eight feet four inches tall, towering over *every man in Europe*!

We can't stereotype cognitive traits either. Men as a whole have better math skills, but Albert Einstein called the mathematician Emmy Noether, "The most significant creative mathematical genius thus far produced since the higher education of women began."[2] Deborah, a judge and prophetess in ancient Israel, possessed more physical courage and skill at war than the warrior Barak. Exceptions to typical male-female traits do exist!

Science struggles to discern whether psychological male-female differences come from biology or culture. Nevertheless, cultural influences play a big part in gender expression. In ancient Greece, men were expected to weep openly at significant events. Homer's writings on Odysseus, the ancient Greek who killed a "cyclops" and helped to win the Trojan War, tell how Odysseus broke down in tears between monster killings. Since the time of Odysseus, Western society has decided that weeping is unmanly. And in fact, men cry about once a month on average to women's more than five times a month. But is that all cultural conditioning, or does testosterone render tear ducts less productive?[3] It can be difficult to tell where nature leaves off and nurture takes over.

As a result, identifying gender differences is a very messy

business. Feminists get angry when differences are emphasized; antifeminists get angry when differences are deemphasized. (I know because I have angered them both!) Beyond angering people, either exaggerating or denying these differences misrepresents the truth. Thank God that we walk into these murky waters with the divine proclamation that God made us *in His image—male and female. In His image* creates commonality between the genders, and *male and female* differentiates them.

In His image. God made us—both genders—in His image to reflect a good God, and therefore, both genders are *good.* Anytime we cite the differences and imply that one gender is inferior, we accuse God of making something that is *not good.*

Male and female. God made us male and female because neither gender completely and adequately represents God. Both genders are good, but both are incomplete without the other. Anytime we minimize the differences between the genders, we deny the need for each gender's uniqueness.

Armed with these two balancing principles, I venture forth to show the complementariness of men and women and the wonderful synergy God had in mind for marriage, the church, and the world—anywhere men and women join together. As I said before, it is a messy business, so allow me to make a mess of things, and please take it all with a dose of humor and compassion.

Biological differences. The Bible calls women the "weaker" sex (1 Peter 3:7). I tried to disprove this by examining the Greek, but *weak* means "weak." And I must admit it is true. Like most women, I am physically weaker than most men, though I like to deny this at times. Ask my family! I have long coveted big, muscular arms. One day while traveling, I

31

set out to bench-press seventy-five pounds in a hotel gym. A strapping young man saw what I was attempting and asked if he could spot me. A bit insulted, I told him I would be *fine*. But I didn't realize that while I could bench-press seventy-five pounds at home, the gym's weight set had a heavier bar.

Once pinned to the bench by seventy-five pounds of weights and a twenty-pound bar, I meekly supplicated the young man: "Young man? Remember how you offered to spot me?" He kindly lifted the ninety-five-pound bar off me. If only I had remembered that "weaker" sex part! Women have about 52 percent of the upper body strength of men.[4] But then, the Proverbs 31 woman "strengthens her arms" (Proverbs 31:17). Benching seventy-five pounds isn't bad!

Humans have twenty-three pairs of chromosomes within each cell; twenty-two of these are alike in both men and women. But the twenty-third pair features two X chromosomes in females and one X and one Y chromosome in males.[5] The lowly Y chromosome sets all the sex differentiation machinery in motion. The funny part is that the Y chromosome is smaller than all the rest.

Tragically, humans can be born with ambiguous genitalia, and the sex of these individuals must be medically assigned. Beyond these rare and perplexing cases, sex change treatments and surgeries have become more commonplace. But because of the chromosomes, adding or removing genitalia and hormones can't really change one's sex. Women still have that XX and men XY.

Hormonal differences. The complex interplay of hormones in male and female bodies can resemble a watercolor painting. Who knows where blue and red end and purple begins? The mixing and blending make the colors inseparable.

Likewise, our hormones wash over one another rather confusingly. But the primary difference between male and female remains: Women have more estrogen, and men have more testosterone. And those hormonal differences lead to differences of temperament.

Men tend to be more physically aggressive and have a higher sex drive.[6] Women are about twice as likely to experience depression.[7] While women are admittedly more neurotic overall, men are more often psychotic. I think it is also safe to say women are more often deceived, but men are more often self-deceived. Men are far more likely to be sociopathic and narcissistic.[8] On the bright side, thanks to higher levels of testosterone, men have more physical courage, whereas more estrogen gives women more natural empathy.

Intellectual differences. Men have greater IQ (intelligence quotient) variance than women. They tend to span the gamut from below-average intelligence to genius, whereas women tend to hover around the average point. Add women's IQs together and average them, and do the same for men, and the numbers match up. Even so, we should avoid placing too much significance on IQ tests, which focus on *measurable* types of intelligence and neglect the subtle types that defy measurement.

As a whole, women are wired for empathy and men for systems. Women tend to be people oriented, while overall, men are more task oriented. One of my vivid childhood memories involves the annual family trip to Florida. Besides being a man, Dad was an engineer by training. When he began to pack the car, a nervous hush came over the family. We knew Dad's wrath might burst forth if we got in the way of his "system." Mom would run around in the house, issuing reminders of

33

toothbrushes and bathing suits, checking individual suitcases, settling little disputes, and calming little fears.

Finally, we would pile into the car. Then Dad would turn around and ask the most embarrassing question of the year: "Does anyone need to tinkle?"

Mom would cringe in empathy. Every kid would blush and say No, wondering when we would be allowed to manage our own bathroom needs. But Dad knew that one overfull bladder would sideline the whole *system* for an entire twenty minutes when we had to pull over at a rest stop.

Since childhood, I have observed that generally, boys are better than girls at math and girls are better than boys at language. Scientists argue about the reasons for this. Some say the overrepresentation of males in math and the sciences stems from social conditioning, period. Some say the differences are intrinsic. Some say they are both. The career choices of men and women in very egalitarian societies, such as Norway, tend to divide similarly to the career choices of less egalitarian societies, implying an innate disposition rather than social conditioning.

Until recently most people agreed that at least one ability is intrinsically superior in males: spatial skills. The average male can imagine the rotation of a three-dimensional object better than the average female. And as it turns out, the popular belief that women are better at multitasking may be true. According to Keith Laws, the research " 'suggests that—in a stressed and complex situation—women are more able to stop and think about what's going on in front of them.' " Child-rearing and home management tend to fling tasks at women simultaneously, whereas in the typical workplace men can operate more sequentially.[9]

Women tend to possess better factual memory. This is why women often play the role of the family chronicler and why when the Smiths are chatting with you, Mrs. Smith edits her husband: "No, Joe and Dana got married in 2002, and Silas was born one year, thirteen days, six hours, forty-three minutes, and twelve seconds later."

Emotional differences. Overall, men more often express emotion physically. Typical male humor tends to be slapstick, involving physical disasters, such as when a man steps on a plank that flies back in his face, while women would cringe with empathy. But don't assume women are necessarily nicer. Women more often engage in verbal aggression. This is why one woman warned, "If I say 'first of all,' run away because I have prepared research, data, charts, and I will destroy you."

Women have more skill at social cues and emotionally relevant information. This begins early, as male infants respond more to objects than people, and female infants respond more readily to the human voice. Into adulthood, it seems that women hear what men say, but men hear what women do. A classic scenario presents itself when a wife has complained about a lack of communication for years, but it doesn't dawn on the husband till the day she moves out.

Women tend to internalize stress, while men tend to externalize it. I like to say it this way: Women attack themselves and end up in therapy; men attack someone else and end up in jail.

Communication flows out of emotion. Men tend to talk more in public, and women talk more at home. In other words, she comes out of her shell as he goes into his cave—Venus and the Cro-Magnon man pass like ships in the night. Women love to talk face-to-face, looking deeply into each other's eyes; men would rather stand side by side while they talk. Likewise, male bonding involves side-by-side activities, such as watching sports or fishing.

Men tend to jump randomly from topic to topic, but women love to exhaust one topic, recognizing the interconnectedness of everything. Women make more supportive noises, such as *uh-huh*, and are more inclined to agree and find commonality. Men tend to prefer an every-man-for-himself approach to socializing and often prefer a bit of debate to keep the energy level high. Women tend to collaborate; men tend to compete.

So there you have it! The mess of male-female differences, which are probably overstated at times and understated at others. But I tried.

Journaling

What do you consider to be your most womanly traits? How does God use those traits to bless others?

_____

_____

_____

_____

_____

_____

_____

_____

_____

Prayer

Oh, genius Designer,

You knew what You were doing when You created a binary race. But God, it is hard for us to blend sometimes. In our marriages, families, churches, and communities, teach us to live and work in harmony, affirming our differences without exaggerating them. Teach us how to respect one another because You respect us. Most of all, teach me as a woman to value my womanliness because You created it. Amen.

---

1. Some definitions are in order. According to Merriam-Webster's online dictionary, *sex* is "either of the two major forms of individuals that occur in many species and that are distinguished respectively as male or female." *Gender* is "the behavioral, cultural, or psychological traits typically associated with one sex."

2. Albert Einstein, "The Late Emmy Noether; Professor Einstein Writes in Appreciation of a Fellow-Mathematician," *New York Times*, May 4, 1935, 12.

3. Lorna Collier, "Why We Cry," *Monitor on Psychology* 45, no. 2 (February 2014): 47.

4. A. Miller, J. MacDougall, M. Tarnopolsky, and D. Sale, "Gender Differences in Strength and Muscle Fiber Characteristics," *European Journal of Applied Physiology and Occupational Physiology* 66, no. 3 (March 1993): 254–262.

5. "How Many Chromosomes Do People Have?" US National Library of Medicine, last modified November 21, 2017, https://ghr.nlm.nih.gov/primer/basics/howmanychromosomes.

6. Roy F. Baumeister, "The Reality of the Male Sex Drive: Is There Anything Good About Men?" *Cultural Animal* (blog), *Psychology Today*, December 8, 2010, https://www.psychologytoday.com/blog/cultural-animal/201012/the-reality-the-male-sex-drive; Dorian Furuna, "Male Aggression: Why Are Men More Violent?" *Homo Aggressivus* (blog), *Psychology Today*, September 22, 2014, https://www.psychologytoday.com/blog/homo-aggressivus/201409/male-aggression.

7. Mayo Clinic Staff, "Depression in Women: Understanding the Gender Gap," Mayo Clinic, last modified January 16, 2016, https://www.mayoclinic.org/diseases-conditions/depression/in-depth/depression/art-20047725?pg=1.

8. Joni E. Johnston, "Female Psychopaths: Are There More Than We Think?"

Human Equation (blog), *Psychology Today*, May 2, 2012, https://www .psychologytoday.com/blog/the-human-equation/201205/female-psychopaths; E. Grijalva, D. A. Newman, L. Tay, M. B. Donnellan, P. D. Harms, R. W. Robins, and T. Yan, "Gender Differences in Narcissism: A Meta-analytic Review," *Psychological Bulletin* 141, no. 2 (March 2015): 267–310.

9. James Morgan, "Women 'Better at Multitasking' Than Men, Study Finds," BBC News, October 24, 2013, http://www.bbc.com/news/science-environment -24645100.

Chapter 4

The Snack That Changed the World

*How the Fall Ruined Everything,
Including the Lives of Women*

Poor Sarah Winchester! In today's currency, the fortune of this nineteenth-century heiress would be worth about five hundred million dollars. But her wealth didn't make her happy; it only added to her misery and horrifying regret. Secret guilt drove Sarah to move from high society in Connecticut to San Jose, California, where she built the famous Winchester mansion—a sprawling labyrinth of chambers designed to house ghosts.

Yes, ghosts.

Windows with thirteen panes, ceilings with thirteen panels, chandeliers with thirteen globes, trap doors, secret passageways, tunnels, stairways leading nowhere, and a bell tower—at Sarah Winchester's command, the workers pieced the weird mansion together. Then every evening at midnight a servant would ring a bell as Sarah entered a special room where she would commune with the spirits of the dead until 2:00 A.M.

Who were these ghosts? As legend goes, they were the American Indians and soldiers killed on the US frontier by bullets from the most popular rifle in America—the Winchester—as in Sarah *Winchester*.

What had brought thousands of dollars to Sarah Winchester had brought thousands of deaths to American Indians and US soldiers and ultimately brought thousands of ghosts into this tormented woman's imagination.

Sarah Winchester's bizarre regret pales in comparison to what Adam and Eve must have experienced as they felt the first chill wind, heard the birds' songs slide into minor keys, and watched wild-eyed animals scamper away in fright. As the sting of death contaminated their perfect world, they knew in the pit of their stomachs that all this horror stemmed from a choice they had both made—the choice to eat the forbidden fruit. Now their disobedience plunged the world into a process of deterioration. If the convulsing sorrow of planet Earth had stretched out before them as we see it stretching back now, they would have died on the spot. But God in His mercy shielded them from a full awareness of the consequences of their sin.

If being responsible for one or a few deaths can ruin a person psychologically, as public-service announcements about texting while driving warn, how much more so with Sarah Winchester's thousands of deaths? And what about Adam and Eve's billions?

Studies show that we often process our regret through excessive rumination; thinking and rethinking the variables that led to the regretted choice. Rumination can be harmful, but the right amount benefits people as they take a moral inventory that can guide them to avoid the same pitfalls over and over.[1] Maybe ruminating a little on what led to Eden's fall will help us to prevent these traps. As we review it, we resonate with each step in the downward spiral because we, too, have taken that twisted descent. Speaking as someone who has read many psychological theories of the human condition, I find Genesis to contain the world's most comprehensive yet the most concise answer to the question of what is wrong with us. For our own sake, let us join the innocent pair in their Eden home for a walk down the dark alley of sin and regret. And since our focus is on Eve, let us allow her to speak:

I had heard from the angels that Satan would not be permitted to follow us through the Garden. Only at the tree of the knowledge of good and evil would he find access to us. Therefore, they warned us, *"Stay away from that tree!"*

If only I had listened! *If only.*

From a distance, I had seen a beautiful creature with iridescent wings. Little did I know Satan had inhabited the creature, called a serpent. In spite of the angels' warnings, I wandered from Adam's side, fighting off my apprehensions by telling myself, *Oh, I can handle it.* If only I had recognized my vulnerability.

If only.

While gazing at the sumptuous, impossibly beautiful fruit, a silvery voice threaded its way into my consciousness: "Did God really say, 'You must not

41

eat from any tree in the garden'?" (Genesis 3:1, NIV).
He had quoted part of what God actually said, which
lent credibility to his question. But he used words to
manipulate me into thinking that somehow God had
deprived us.

I should have turned and run for my life; but I en-
gaged him, countering his statement with, "We may
eat fruit from the trees in the garden, but God did say,
'You must not eat fruit from the tree that is in the middle of the garden, and *you must not touch it*, or you will
die' " (verses 2, 3, NIV; emphasis added).

Then words that should have terrified me shot from
the creature's mouth: "You will not surely die. For God
knows that in the day you eat of it your eyes will be
opened, and you will be like God, knowing good and
evil" (verse 4).

"You will not surely die." "God lied," he said. "He
lied because He knows you will get special knowledge
from this fruit, and you will take your rightful place as
equal to Him. Motivated by jealousy, possessiveness,
and insecurity, God has imposed this stifling restriction upon you; a restriction you must break if you will
ever find freedom."

He then plucked the fruit, placed it in my hands,
and pointed to the fact that even though I had pre-
dicted that touching it would bring death, I was fine.
*Eating it won't bring any more harm to you than touch-
ing it*, he insinuated. And thus he lured me onward.
Mesmerized, I seized the fruit, digging my teeth into
the smooth flesh; its juices exploding with flavor. My
whole body began to shake with a strange exhilaration.

"Adam! Adam!" I called.

Adam's eyes clouded over in sorrow. He knew I had fallen, but he couldn't stand the thought of separation. Finally, he seized and ate the fruit, vowing to die with me rather than live without me.

Initially, for a few seconds, we both seemed to feel a sense of exhilaration. Then suddenly something shifted like a tectonic plate within us. The change was more than physical. We felt a sense of defilement and a corresponding deep horror. Dread crept in like fog as the true gravity of our sin settled upon us. The robes of light that had clothed us dissolved away until we clutched at our naked bodies in shame. That shame, so dark, so horrifying—there are no words for it.

We quickly covered our bodies with fig leaves, assuring ourselves that we could earn back God's favor. But our self-assurance crumbled when He came to find us. Fear consumed us and we hid. Then the blaming began: Adam blamed me, and I blamed the serpent creature. The man who had only a short time before given up all that he held dear rather than be separated from me, hoped I would bear the retribution in his place.

The Bible plainly tells us that the man wasn't deceived (1 Timothy 2:14). He intentionally gave the fair earth over to the enemy rather than be separated from the woman he loved. But human love when separated from its divine source dies quickly. In the cool of the very same day, Adam blamed his wife in the hope that she would die instead of him. This chilling fact puts a big, ugly exclamation point at the end of the sentence about sin's impact on human nature.

Because of sin, our self-love displaces love of others.

In the face of the crumbling earthly kingdom, God instituted His plan of salvation and preached the gospel. Turning to the serpent, He promised that "enmity" would separate his kingdom from God's, that "enmity" would "bruise" his head, and that he would "bruise His heel" (Genesis 3:15). In essence, "enmity" would destroy the enemy, the serpent Satan.

God followed this good news with the not-so-good news of the consequences of sin for Eve and Adam respectively. These judgments carry very heavy implications for the struggles of the men and the women on our forlorn planet. Beginning with the woman, God said,

> "I will greatly multiply your sorrow and your
>   conception;
> In pain you shall bring forth children;
> Your desire shall be for your husband,
> And he shall rule over you" (verse 16).

Moving on to the man, He said,

> "Cursed is the ground for your sake;
> In toil you shall eat of it
> All the days of your life.
> Both thorns and thistles it shall bring forth for you,
> And you shall eat the herb of the field.
> In the sweat of your face you shall eat bread
> Till you return to the ground,
> For out of it you were taken;
> For dust you are,

And to dust you shall return" (verses 16–19).

Let's distill the respective curses of Eve and Adam to their essential points:

- The woman would suffer in bearing children.
- She would "desire" her husband.
- He would "rule over" her.
- The man would toil away on cursed ground to survive.
- He would exert himself and "sweat" as he struggled to provide.
- He would ultimately die anyway.

Bible students propose two options regarding these judgments: They are either *prescriptive* or *descriptive*. Was God prescribing punishment or simply describing consequences? Before you answer too quickly, consider that the story unrolls like what Old Testament scholar Richard M. Davidson calls a "legal process." He says, "Following the legal interrogation and establishment of guilt, God pronounces the sentence in the form of curses . . . and judgments."[2]

But as in all human experience, a great controversy raged. On the post-Fall earth, two things competed for the upper hand—God's just and merciful consequences for sin, and the devil's unjust and merciless perversion of God's justice. Appropriately, the woman would now have limitations on the freedom she had abused. Sin had made the world a dangerous place where she and her children would need protection, and God organized the family to bring about that protection.

But as time unfolded, Satan took Eve's vulnerable state and ran with it; mocking God's reasonable consequences by taking them far beyond the limits of justice; heaping upon womankind extraordinary suffering, far out of proportion to Eve's sin; and then claiming God had ordained it.

Note that an important reality surrounds this issue with the golden frame of redemptive love. In God, curses become blessings. God has a wonderful power to take the very worst things, even the things we bring upon ourselves, and make them the best things. The bitter consequences of sin can be a gateway to intimacy with the Sin Pardoner. Through Eve's care of her children; through her dependency upon her husband; through Adam's hard, sweaty work; and even through his dying, God would find access to humanity and ultimately lead us to something even better than the Eden we lost. When we open our clenched hands, God always gives us something better—something better than what we have, and something better than what we deserve. He's just that good.

In the absence of this deep knowledge of God's character, Adam and Eve must have felt ice-cold despair as they saw armed angels stationed around the tree of life. That tree had provided an unending supply of vitality, but to partake of it now that their very natures had withered with corruption would immortalize sin itself. Mighty, glittering angels turned them away, which pierced their hearts with the reality of the privileges lost. Adding to their despair, God told them that they must leave their Eden home in spite of their desperate pleas to stay. No one knows in the moment of temptation how terrible the consequences of yielding will be.

If only, if only, if only.

They didn't yet fully know how God would give them

"beauty for ashes,
The oil of joy for mourning,
The garment of praise for the spirit of heaviness;
That they may be called trees of righteousness,
The planting of the Lord, that He may be glorified"
   (Isaiah 61:3).

Journaling
When you think of deep regret, what life experience comes to mind? How has God encouraged you in spite of it?

_____

_____

_____

_____

_____

_____

_____

_____

_____

_____

_____

_____

Prayer

Blessed Redeemer,

You turn curses into blessings, or I would be under a curse right now. Make the consequences of my sins the entry point where Your grace floods my life, pushing out regret and discouragement until I have fully internalized the story of redemption. Then strengthen me to share with other regretful ones the God that will dry their tears and give them another chance. Amen.

---

1. Melanie Greenberg, "The Psychology of Regret," *The Mindful Self-Express* (blog), *Psychology Today*, May 16, 2012, https://www.psychologytoday.com/blog /the-mindful-self-express/201205/the-psychology-regret.

2. Davidson, "Headship, Submission, and Equality in Scripture."

Chapter 5

Expensive Clothes

*The Heart-, Mind-, and Life-Altering
Righteousness of Christ*

The press reports what men have known for years:
Women spend a heap of money on clothes. One
study from Great Britain showed that the average woman
forks over nearly $111,000 in a lifetime on an array of items,
including 271 pairs of shoes, 185 dresses, and 145 bags. This
would be less shocking if it weren't also true that 60 percent
of women admit to struggling to find something to wear on
a daily basis.[1] The tragic cry "I have nothing to wear!" has
ascended from womankind since time immemorial.

The psychology of dress says that nothing looks as attrac-
tive as when you try it on for the first time. This novelty
factor may fuel our overspending, but the deeper motive
is our desire to *look good*. Maybe putting ourselves in Eve's
place for a moment will check our appetite for newer and
better dresses because, after all, she wore the same outfit every day. And maybe if we are clothed in the righteousness

49

symbolized by Eve's garment we will feel a sense of security that will ultimately tame our runaway clothing budgets. *Looking good* before the throne of God will make it less important to *look good* elsewhere.

I'm talking to myself here. My primary female role model—a.k.a. my mother—was a beauty, in my humble opinion. Dad held the sales manager position for the largest corporation in our state, and he provided her with a generous clothing budget. Often they would attend fancy events; Mom would pull out of the closet one of her glittering gowns, spend some extra time on her hair and makeup, and emerge from her dressing room looking like a goddess. I think this felt like abandonment to me, as if she were leaving my earthly world and going to her own preternatural realm.

Throughout my childhood, I had a recurring dream in which I would come upon her singing a haunting melody while dressed in blue chiffon, diamonds, and sapphires; her black-brown eyes would be fixed on some distant point. I would try to get her attention with my usual "Mommy! Mommy!" and she would look past me as if I weren't there. I felt the same way when she wore her evening gowns and left with Dad as she walked out holding his arm. I saw the idea conveyed perfectly that a woman's expensive clothes got her into privileged places, places I could not go unless I had the right clothes.

How about the presence of a holy God? Would that be a privileged place? Most certainly. And the clothing God gives us gains us admittance there. Isn't it remarkable that at the very core of the gospel we find this clothing metaphor? And God doesn't mind either, for He gives us the finest garments we will ever wear, purchased at an infinite price by Him, given as free gifts to us. Those garments are the white robes of Jesus' righteousness.

Shortly after God's pronouncements of judgment upon the shame-filled Adam and Eve, He did something highly symbolic and yet totally functional at the same time. "Also for Adam and his wife the LORD God made tunics of skin, and clothed them" (Genesis 3:21). Now that the changing weather would chill bare legs at times and send a dry wind that might chap their skin, they needed substantial coverings. Beyond this, in their sinful state, the very heavenly love that they had once welcomed looked threatening to them: the holiness of a loving God would sear their souls. They needed a shelter from that storm too.

Imagine how Eve might recount the story:

The entrance of sin changed everything. Nature immediately shifted from harmony and order to discord and disorder. The animals that had so recently eaten from our hands fled at the sound of our footsteps on the path. From raccoons to wallabies, they hid in their holes and nests, darting out only to find food or mates.

I loved one fawn in particular. She used to play with me in the brook, then nestle her head in the crook of my neck while we lay in a bed of grass. Now she sprinted into the woods in terror, tail bobbing frantically until she found safety in the darkness.

But it was a lamb I cherished that was among those that became my covering. In horror, I watched as God's mighty hands grasped her, somehow slitting her neck until the life drained out in a little crimson pool on the ground. I thought perhaps some of God's own

51

tears mingled with her blood. Then He tore the skin away from her lifeless body and from it and other skins formed a beautiful, sturdy garment.

I could barely see through my brimming eyes, but I stared anyway. I felt I owed it to my little lamb. My covering had cost the life of something dear to me, and I began to comprehend how this spoke of what it cost to cover my sin.

Adam and I stood there, fig leaves curling in on themselves, drying against our skin. "You must take those off," God said, "for your covering must be from Me alone." Fig leaves are very scratchy and felt like tree bark against our skin, yet the prospect of being naked before God filled us both with a wordless dread. Together we took a deep breath, closed our eyes, and quickly removed the leaves as we felt a surging tide of shame well up inside. The chill air against our skin quickly affected the temperature of our bodies, and we stood shaking in an effort to stay warm. Or was it shame that prompted the shaking? Perhaps both. At any rate, we shuddered, thinking we had come to our end.

Suddenly, a soft warmth fell upon us from head to toe. God was dressing His children, just like a mother dressing her baby. As the skins draped around our chilled shoulders and down, down to our legs and arms, we began to feel a sense of deep relief. We may not have been in our right minds, but we were clothed again!

As the man and woman clutched their new garments, they began to understand the central teaching of the Bible, which theologians call justification by faith. The righteousness of

Jesus, which the skin garments of Eden symbolized, meant more to them than they realized. As Adam and Eve so painfully witnessed, their covering demanded the death of One very dear to them. The serpent would bruise the "Seed" of the woman, the Messiah, as He died the death that sinful human beings deserved. Through this death, He could cover them in His very own robe of pure, sinless righteousness, and they could once again stand before a holy God without fear of condemnation.

Today we can stand before God in the same robe, knowing that He sees us not in our sin, but *in Christ*. When Adam chose to sin, he effectively gave up his position as head of the unfallen human race. Fortunately, God Himself took it back from the usurper as Jesus positioned Himself to become "the last Adam" (1 Corinthians 15:45). If God had His way, every man, woman, and child from that point forward would accept the righteousness of His Son and become part of the new humanity in Christ, putting on those beautiful robes purchased for us at such cost.

Those who receive the gift accept more than a change of status. Once we allow God to clothe us in these expensive garments, they act reflexively to transform our thoughts and feelings. As women, we understand how much our outer garments can influence our inner state.

One of the most troubling and pervasive consequences of sin is a baseline sense of shame—a shame for which we continually try to compensate with all kinds of fig leaves: legalistic fig leaves based on our religious works; relational fig leaves in which we try to derive value and worthiness from relationships; materialistic fig leaves through which we try to bury our shame under mountains of possessions;

narcissistic fig leaves by which vanity and pride rule our wills. The list is endless. Made in the image of a Creator God, we are quite creative!

Desperately throughout life, we deny our sin because to see it in its full strength would bring upon us a shame response of such intensity that our hearts would stop. Remember that Jesus died of the physical effects of this shame, which He experienced as if it were His own. The horrifying weight of sin pressing upon Him while the holy hatred of sin burned in His Shekinah heart caused an internal decompensation that ultimately broke His heart and ended His life.

We undergo our own version of this as we taste the cup of shame Jesus drank to the dregs. The horror of that experience will lead us to throw all our energy into avoiding it unless some foundational security fortifies us to bear it.

The Messiah's righteousness is that security. When we know that in spite of our sin He forgives us, that He reverses our condemnation, and that He unfailingly loves us, we begin to release our defenses and learn to rest in His goodness rather than our own. Then He can reveal our hidden sins so that we can say, "I don't need that in my life"; sin by sin, He can cleanse our souls and shape us into His love.

My sisters, "put on your beautiful garments" (Isaiah 52:1). We are going out tonight. You will be on the arm of the most dashing of men, the Second Adam, the Prince of Peace. He will usher you into the most elite company—the angelic host, who will sing in joy at your arrival. There before the holy God you will stand, secure in His Son's love and righteousness, the Father who gave that Son for you smiling down in approval because you did the one thing He asked above all others.

You wore the garment He made for you. You put on His expensive clothes.

Journaling

What are your favorite fig leaves? In other words, how do you try to fix yourself apart from God?

Prayer

Divine Dressmaker,

Thank You for this beautiful garment of righteousness that comes as a free gift to me, yet at infinite cost to Yourself. Thank You that even though I often turn to my scratchy old fig leaves for covering, I can always return to the rest, comfort, and security found in You. Help me revert back less and less. Help me not to fear standing naked before You. Help me to wear this robe of righteousness, believing that You will forgive and cleanse me from all sin, so I can stand in the presence of a holy God in You. Amen.

1. Daily Mail Reporter, "Women Spend £80K on Clothes in a Lifetime and Still Complain They Have Nothing to Wear," DailyMail.com, July 5, 2012, http://www.dailymail.co.uk/news/article-2169005/Women-spend-80K-clothes-lifetime-STILL-complain-wear.html.

Chapter 6

The Real Curse of Women

How the Consequences of Sin Become a Blessing

God is the Great Recycler. He watches over this demon-ravaged planet, searching out opportunities to turn bastards into great men and to turn curses into blessings. Even the curses that we wandering, disobedient sinners bring upon ourselves can be molded into blessings by His mighty, compassionate, second-chance hands, making us more blessed in the end than we would have been had we never fallen. As author Ellen White writes, "By His life and His death, Christ has achieved even *more than recovery* from the ruin wrought through sin."[1] God doesn't just piece things back together, He masterpieces things back together.

And God would take the pieces of Eve's life and make a masterpiece of His love. But for the time being, Eve was broken. I am sure His words seared themselves into her memory: *"Pain in childbearing. . . . Desire will be for your husband, . . . he will rule over you"* (Genesis 3:16, NIV). She must have mulled them over many times: *"Rabah rabah 'itstsabown herown 'etseb yalad ben tĕshuwqah 'iysh mashal."*

> "I will greatly multiply your sorrow
>   and your conception;
> In pain you shall bring forth children;
> Your desire shall be for your husband,
> And he shall rule over you" (verse 16).

Notice the language: God said, "*I* will greatly multiply your sorrow." God wanted Eve to see at least the first of this three-part sentence as proceeding from Him. This doesn't mean that God would personally interpose to inflict pain each time she bore a child. God rules over all things and sometimes speaks of things He allows as things He actively *does*. For instance, He said to Satan regarding Job, "You incited *Me* against him," as if God directly afflicted Job (Job 2:3; emphasis added). Yet the account clearly shows Satan doing the afflicting.

Often in the Bible, God takes responsibility for the things that Satan, nature, or people do simply because for Him, who is all powerful, sovereign, and the Source and Sustainer of all things, even to allow something is to be responsible for it. Eve's sufferings would happen on His watch. Therefore, even if He simply allowed a natural process to unfold, He laid claim to it as His own doing.

This means that it must have been a blessing because God's curses become blessings in Christ. But I am getting ahead of myself. Let us examine the three parts of Eve's punishment, one by one.

Pain in childbearing. The first of the three points summons up images of a woman shrieking her way through the unspeakable pain of labor. Let me assure anyone who has never experienced this particular agony that it is shriek worthy. Being an all-natural, granola type, I gave birth to two children without the help of anesthesia, and I really, really get the part about *pain* in childbearing. But notice the expansiveness of the statement: "I will greatly multiply your sorrow and your conception; in pain you shall bring forth children."

There are actually two parts to this: (1) multiplied sorrow in conception and (2) bringing forth children in pain. Scholars believe the statements together refer to both the physical pain of labor and the larger picture of all that is entailed in the bearing of children. I agree. Physical reality has a way of metaphorizing spiritual reality. In my experience, the agony of childbirth—as nail biting as it is—pales in comparison to the often heartbreaking, drawn-out process of "birthing" a solid, saved human being.

The first piece of Eve's threefold curse applies to *everything* about women's childbearing role that brings pain and grief. For instance, the physical pain of women's reproductive capacity doesn't begin and end with childbirth. What about menstrual cramps? What about menopause? And childbearing doesn't refer only to biological children. Women most often care for every dependent person in the family system, including disabled loved ones, aging parents, and the stray cats that come to the door.

Here's my own master list of the "in pain you shall bring forth children" experience that falls to the lot of women all over the world. Feel free to add your own entries:

1. Often pubescent females experience lowered confidence over body image.[2]

2. Premenstrual tension, cramps, and mood changes affect most women.

3. Sometimes premenstrual syndrome (PMS) is so bad it becomes a diagnosable and debilitating disorder called premenstrual dysphoric disorder (PMDD).

4. Monthly blood loss predisposes women to iron deficiency.

5. Pregnancy itself can deplete a woman's mineral stores.

6. Women can develop ovarian cysts, endometriosis, pelvic inflammatory disease, cervical cancer, prolapsed uterus, and a host of other reproductive diseases.

7. About 830 women per day die in childbirth worldwide. Ninety-nine percent of these are in developing countries.[3]

8. Even healthy childbirth leaves marks on women's bodies, including but not limited to visible stretch marks; changes in bowels, vagina, breasts, fat distribution; and the general acquisition of "elephant skin stomach syndrome" (my own term).

9. Women are the primary caregivers for children, even though more and more of them are the primary breadwinners too.

10. Even though women are the sole breadwinners in four out of ten households, they still do the majority of the housework.[4]

11. The fact that women bear and care for children reduces their investment in their careers and makes them less desirable in the eyes of many employers.

12. Women are not just more likely to sacrifice their careers to care for children, they are more likely to care for aging parents too.[5]

Desire will be for your husband. The second part of Eve's three-part sentence is the most difficult to understand. What did God mean when He said, "Your desire shall be for your husband"? Sexual desire? Desire for approval? Desire for control? Scholars debate this mysterious wording and come up with very different interpretations.[6] *Teshuqua*, the Hebrew word for "desire," only appears two other times in the Old Testament. It describes sin's "desire" for Cain in Genesis 4:7 and the bridegroom's desire for the bride in Song of Solomon 7:10. Considering all three contexts in which the word appears, it simply means a deep longing directed at a specific object—in Eve's case, Adam.

In the broadest sense, women crave the approval of, and the intimacy with, the men in their lives. For some, this means fathers and brothers; for some, it includes husbands. Some of this stems from women's generally relational nature. Richly gifted with relational intelligence, we tend to desire a deeper level of closeness than men do.

I have counseled scores of married couples, and the wives almost always desire more emotional intimacy than the husbands. I engage in a quick survey, asking, "How would you rate your marriage on a scale of one to ten?" Almost without exception, the woman rates the marriage lower than the man does.

This desire also flows naturally from the pain and toil in childbearing. With so many needy ones depending upon us, with so much pain and struggle involved in carrying their burdens, women naturally long for the support of a strong, stable figure.

Women have, overall, lower self-esteem than men,[7] and much of it is tied to physical appearance. Women seek plastic surgery about nine times more often than men do.[8] Some of these surgeries are attempts to patch together a broken self-concept through attaining physical perfection and sex appeal. We keep the diet industry afloat too: up to 50 percent of women are on a diet at any given time.[9] Nine out of ten eating disorder patients are female,[10] and most eating disorders are diet and thinness related.

In addition, we women tend to define ourselves by our connections. Studies show that while men typically derive self-worth from their abilities and their achievements, women seem to gain self-worth more often through their relationships.[11] Even when men do derive self-worth through their relationships, it has more to do with the enhancement of their social status, whereas women derive self-worth from the relationship itself.[12]

All these factors create a desire that makes women inclined to attach to another. In God's ideal post-Fall plan, this relational orientation would actually facilitate healthy bonding. The wife would cope with the dangers of a sinful world by leaning on the protection and affection of a servant-leader husband. She would, in a unique and gifted way, facilitate the relationships within the entire family system.

He will rule over you. Eve's vulnerability in bearing children, plus her longing desire for affection and approval, would give Adam a power advantage, which flows naturally into the third aspect of Eve's sentence: He would rule over her. According to Paul, because "Adam was formed first, then Eve" and because "Adam was not deceived, but the woman being deceived, fell into transgression," Eve would submit and Adam would rule (1 Timothy 2:13, 14).

But this would be a protective rule rather than an

autocratic one. The world had morphed into a dangerous place where women and children needed a shielding figure to keep them safe. And the power struggles that would arise as a result of sin necessitated a final decision maker. In designating man as the head, God was simply being pragmatic.

Note that of all the biblical references to wives submitting, not one tells the husband to *make* the wife submit. They each enlist the wife's voluntary submission. This implies a type of leadership that would encourage a desire to submit. When a man forces his authority on his wife, he kills the spirit of true submission and brings in a spirit that is foreign to God's freedom-granting character of love. Many a miserable woman can attest to this.

Even in its best form, this arrangement would be a disappointment and a compromise after the first couple enjoyed perfect equality of power before the Fall. God must have assigned the subjugation of women with much hesitancy, given its potentially devastating effects. Marriage functions best in a configuration of equality. The healthiest families are team led, with the leadership team pooling the gifts and abilities of both members.

When one member of a dyad makes all the decisions, possesses all the wisdom, and wields all the power, the relationship begins to resemble a parent-child bond. Often the first thing to suffer is the sexual aspect of the relationship (most sexually normal people don't become attracted to their mothers, fathers, or children). The romantic bond between a man and a woman thrives much better on an eye-to-eye level than top down.[13] Although men seem to thrive more on respect and women on affection (Ephesians 5:33), both genders need both sides of the love coin. And

63

the woman ideally admires her husband as an equal rather than a superior.

Many a woman, knowing she possessed a mind and a soul equal to her husband's, but bound by convention to let him do all the decision making, has silently rebelled in a form of passive-aggressive manipulation, such as characterized by Toula's mother in the movie *My Big Fat Greek Wedding*. She said, "The man is the head, but the woman is the neck. And she can turn the head any way she wants."[14] Because of this devious maneuvering, couples that claim to exemplify female subjugation are sometimes far from it in private. A wife can become a silent, behind-the-scenes, tantrum-throwing micromanager.

With all its liabilities, we are led to ask whether this subjugated state was given as the ordained configuration of a God-centered marriage. Or was it an emergency measure to cope with the exigencies of Adam and Eve's sinful, selfish state? Clearly, it was an emergency arrangement to help maintain harmony in the short term while striving for Eden's original design in the long term. We strive for Eden in our food choices, our treatment of animals, our connection to nature, and our holy living. Why not also in our relationships with one another? How about with all three parts of the sentence Eve heard in the Garden?

Even as God spoke the words, He began to put cosmic wheels in motion that would bring the fallen pair as close as possible to their original state of harmony and equality. He would recycle the suffering caused by sin into an opportunity to know Him, the sin-pardoning Savior. And through an intimate connection to Him, men and women would learn to discern between true servant leadership and the enemy's counterfeit.

Journaling

How have you seen the three parts of Genesis 3:16 play out in your own life?

_____

_____

_____

_____

_____

_____

_____

_____

Prayer

O heavenly Head of humanity,

Humanity's fall into sin has broken us and put us in less-than-ideal circumstances. Teach me how to navigate through this situation with dignity and grace, as Your beloved daughter. Give me good boundaries so that I can care for others without enabling them. Help me to accept my normal desires for approval without lapsing into approval addiction. Give me a spirit of godly submission to You, first and foremost, and then to others as You lead. Amen.

---

1. Ellen G. White, *The Desire of Ages* (Mountain View, CA: Pacific Press®, 1940), 25; emphasis added.

2. Barbara M. Newman and Philip R. Newman, *Development Through Life: A Psychosocial Approach*, 9th ed. (Belmont, CA: Wadsworth, 2006), 303.

3. World Health Organization, "Maternal Mortality," fact sheet, last updated November 2016, http://www.who.int/mediacentre/factsheets/fs348/en/.

4. Abigail Bessler, "Even Today, Women Still Do Most of the Housework and Childcare," Think Progress, June 18, 2014, http://thinkprogress.org /economy/2014/06/18/3450416/women-housework-childcare/.

5. Paula Span, "Work, Women and Caregiving," *The New Old Age* (blog), *New York Times*, November 21, 2013, https://newoldage.blogs.nytimes .com/2013/11/21/work-women-and-caregiving/.

6. One interpretation, popular in complementarian circles, says that the word *desire* means a desire "for control," as in, the woman wanted control of the man (but he would "rule over" her instead). Applying this interpretation to the two other passages that use this word rules it out, though, because that would mean that the bride in Song of Solomon said of the bridegroom, "I am my beloved's, and his desire is to control me." Interpreting the word as emotional and sexual longing does no violence to the interpretation of the other two verses, so it is the more consistent interpretation.

7. American Psychological Association, "Self-Esteem Gender Gap More Pronounced in Western Countries," news release, January 4, 2016, http://www.apa .org/news/press/releases/2016/01/self-esteem-gender.aspx.

8. Martin Donohoe, "Cosmetic Surgery Past, Present, and Future: Scope, Ethics, and Policy," Medscape, November 6, 2006, https://www.medscape.com /viewarticle/542448_2.

9. Tammy Dray, "Facts and Statistics About Dieting," LiveStrong.com, last updated July 18, 2017, https://www.livestrong.com/article/390541-facts-statistics -about-dieting/.

10. "Statistics: How Many People Have Eating Disorders?" ANRED, accessed November 28, 2017, https://www.anred.com/stats.html.

11. See, for instance, R. A. Josephs, H. R. Markus, and R. W. Tafarodi, "Gender and Self-Esteem," *Journal of Personal Social Psychology* 63, no. 3 (September 1992): 391–402.

12. T. Kwang, E. E. Crockett, D. T. Sanchez, and W. B. Swann Jr., "Men Seek Social Standing, Women Seek Companionship: Sex Differences in Deriving Self-Worth From Relationships," *Psychological Science* 24, no. 7 (July 2013): 1142–1150.

13. Our society's current obsession with bondage and discipline and sadomasochism (BDSM) interestingly enough features one person in complete control of another.

14. *My Big Fat Greek Wedding*, directed by Joel Zwick (Burbank, CA: Warner Home Video, 2003), DVD.

Chapter 7

Where Is Your Head?

*The Vast Difference
Between Servant Leadership
and Selfish Dictatorship*

My housemates and I kept throwing away inedible loaves of bread we tried to make. Seized with the notion that we should bake our own bread, we ventured forth with inadequate knowledge of the complex science behind a good loaf. After several dry, crumbly, flat attempts ended up in the trash, we reevaluated. Someone heard that the addition of salt would help regulate the yeast, even out the crumb, and also improve the flavor. Voilà! A little salt made all the difference.

Introducing a new variable, however humble that variable may be, can sometimes transform a discouraging situation. This also applies to relationships. For example, I once worked for a company under a very abusive, manipulative boss and a kind, unselfish supervisor. The boss would harass the women, mercilessly criticize those who got in his way, and generally create chaos. A competitive, uncooperative spirit hovered around him like a swarm of flies, subtly leading the employees to distrust and betray one another.

When the boss flew overseas on a business trip, the supervisor would step in and everything would shift into a peaceful mode. Employees would begin to cooperate again. Stress levels lowered. Smiles replaced worry lines, and all was well. A new variable—a change of leadership—altered the relationships and even the people themselves.

We would all like to go back to the peace and harmony of Eden, where Adam and Eve never fought or even disagreed. God would like us to strive for Eden too; but we will have to introduce a new variable—a type of leader who will calm the system. Let us see what happens to the punishment upon womankind in Genesis 3:16 when we add a servant-leader husband. We can't, with loyalty to Scripture, omit servant leadership without completely misrepresenting God's plan for marriage.

Let me explain. In sketching out the marital relationship, the apostle Paul said, "Wives, submit to your own husbands, as is fitting in the Lord" (Colossians 3:18). Notice something here. This submission can't possibly be mindless, because the wives must utilize their faculties to discern whether their submission is "fitting in the Lord." What determines whether it is "fitting in the Lord"? The next verse clarifies this: "Husbands, love your wives and do not be bitter toward them" (verse 19). A wife can safely submit to a husband who loves her as Christ loves her, knowing that no incongruity would exist between her husband's will and God's.

This was the ideal God had in mind when He uttered Eve's three-part sentence for sin. The husband would exemplify

Christ Himself, and the dance between the spouses would resemble the wooing process in which Christ loves His church and ultimately wins her perfect trust. "Husbands, love your wives, just as Christ also loved the church and gave Himself for her" (Ephesians 5:25). Husbands (and in the broadest sense, all men) have been assigned the task of representing Jesus to the women in their lives. There outside the Garden, God set Adam and Eve up to act out the drama of the ages—God's quest for humanity. Adam would play Jesus; the woman, His bride.

Curses become blessings in Christ

Notice that God gives respective tasks to the husband and the wife, which they fulfill in obedience to Him. He makes neither husband nor wife responsible for the other's task. He doesn't say, "Husbands, make your wives submit," or "Wives, make your husbands love you." Neither can choose obedience for the other. Far from leading to mind control, these injunctions, when freely chosen, lead to submission to God and then to mutual love and submission to one another.

With servant leadership in place, the Genesis 3:16 picture shifts from one that would open the floodgates for the abuse and oppression of women to one that reveals God's self-giving love and would ultimately produce much happier husbands and wives. While a self-serving leader uses his power to lift himself up, a servant-leader uses his power to lift others up. A self-serving leader loves to dominate those under him, but a servant-leader loves to elevate those under him. A self-serving leader lives to enrich an insecure but inflated ego, but a servant-leader lives to pour out his life to enrich others.

The great Servant-Leader—the Bridegroom, Jesus—came in search of His wandering lover, marching forward to a hideous cross where "He poured out His soul unto death" (Isaiah 53:12). Through Christ, fallen, sinful men can also pour themselves out and lift up those around them.

Notice the downward-pouring motion of love in this passage: "Let this mind be in you which was also in Christ Jesus, who, being in the form of God, did not consider it robbery to be equal with God, but made Himself of no reputation, taking the form of a bondservant, and coming in the likeness of men. And being found in appearance as a man, He humbled Himself and became obedient to the point of death, even the death of the cross" (Philippians 2:5–8). From "equal with God" to "the death of the cross," Jesus plunged from the heights of heaven into our hell to lift us back up to heaven. Like an excavator's shovel, He dug into the depths of our lost condition to get underneath us, so He could lift from below.

Notice what comes next: "*Therefore* God also has highly exalted Him and given Him the name which is above every name, that at the name of Jesus every knee should bow, of those in heaven, and of those on earth, and of those under the earth, and that every tongue should confess that Jesus Christ is Lord, to the glory of God the Father" (verses 9–11; emphasis added).

Therefore, God has exalted Jesus. Why? Because He lowered Himself! In other words, Jesus, possessing all the privileges, power, and prerogatives of God, sacrificed those things so that God could exalt Him on the basis of love *alone*. He could have clung to His status. He didn't. He took our humanity and died feeling the burning shame of a trillion criminals because serving and saving us mattered more than His status. But He earned His status back by surrendering it at the cross! He earned the right to ask us to submit to Him by first submitting Himself to the harrowing process of saving us. In God's plan, submission is always based on the sacrificial love of the one submitted to.

The only kind of submission possible apart from self-sacrificing love is a self-centered submission of fear that ultimately compromises freedom and individuality. How dare we propose a craven, degrading submission of wives to husbands? How contrary to God's character and to the gospel itself! Jesus died for our freedom. Why would He then prescribe a state of bondage in marriage that ultimately destroys freedom and individuality?

When we add the servant-leader element to Eve's Genesis 3:16 sentence, we see an entirely different picture than the one often presented: We see a woman enduring the pain and difficulty of bearing and caring for biological and spiritual children, with the support and love of a man who values her ministry and encourages her development. We see a woman longing for close affinity, secure bonding, and deep intimacy, and receiving it freely from a man filled with the love of Christ, which makes the longing fulfilled rather than frustrated. We see a man leading his family in such a way as to place his wife in equality with him, considering her a partner rather than a peon in the family firm and a team player in the game of life. And through all this, we see God's ultimate plan for marriage, that through the clear channel of her godly husband, the woman will see a revelation of the Servant of servants, Jesus. In this way, the curse on a woman becomes a blessing through which the love of God can transform her soul and help her bear a testimony of His power to redeem the worst of situations.

At least some of you are thinking, *Yeah, right. The man in my life is certainly not a servant-leader, so I guess I'm doomed.*

Not so fast. Of course, this is a difficult and sad situation; it is a situation many if not most women must face. But does it not help you to love and trust God more, just knowing that He *wants* better things for you? That He wants the husbands, fathers, uncles, and brothers in your life to protect your vulnerabilities rather than exploit them? That He wants you to enjoy individuality, equality, and perfect, joyful freedom? And that He bids you come to Him who is the ultimate Servant-Leader, for He is your true Husband (see Isaiah 54:5).

Doesn't it comfort you to know that God's kind of submission is essentially a trust based on love, rather than mere compliance based on fear? That He only asks you to submit your heart to those who have sacrificed for you? That He who has all power doesn't ask you to submit mindlessly but out of thoughtful adoration? And won't that understanding help buoy your spirits, even if you are unfortunate enough to have what Abigail called a "son of Belial" husband (1 Samuel 25:25)?

It is sad but true that most men don't embody this servant leadership. Often the resulting vacuum sucks in an authoritarian counterfeit that completely misrepresents the character of God and undermines the growth of humanity into His image. Husbands who exercise arbitrary control often depict the enemy of God much more effectively than they represent God Himself. This becomes extremely vexing in a religious context where such men misuse Scripture in an attempt to validate un-Christlike domination.

These men's wives suffer as everything within them rises up against the abuse of power, now and then spilling out in words and actions, but sometimes remaining locked inside like a hot, festering boil. Because women tend to internalize problems, such a home stressor will often result in physical or mental illness. Such women must pray earnestly to know when to comply with the resident tyrant; but their acquiescence will always be superficial and behavioral as it pertains to that tyrant, for he makes true, heartfelt submission impossible.

More than a century ago, Bible scholar and family life expert Ellen White said, "[Man] must be under the rule of Christ that he may represent the relation of Christ to the church. If he is a coarse, rough, boisterous, egotistical, harsh, and overbearing man, *let him never utter the word that the husband is the head of the wife*, and that she must submit to him in everything; for he is not the Lord, *he is not the husband* in the true significance of the term."[1]

God wanted to give women servant-leader husbands, fathers, brothers who were these things in the *true significance of the terms*. Unfortunately, the story of womankind has been rewritten by the millions of men who have not been true to their calling.

God turns curses into blessings. The God-given new variable of a servant-leader takes the Genesis 3:16 punishment and transforms it into a means of uplifting womankind. That's all well and good; but for the most part, it has not come to be. In the next chapter, to understand ourselves better and to empathize with our sisters worldwide, we will look briefly at the lot of women globally and see how the enemy has turned God's blessing back into a curse.

Journaling

What is your response to seeing how Jesus sacrificed for you, invested in you, and loved you infinitely before He asked you to follow Him?

_____

_____

_____

_____

_____

_____

_____

_____

Prayer

Dear Divine Servant-Leader,

It is so good to see that the codependency, enabling, and doormat existence so many women think is Your will for them is as far from it as the east is from the west. It is good to see that Your kind of leadership stands in sharp contrast to the top-down oppression that is the world's idea of leadership. Now that I see this, I realize that surrendering and submitting to You will insure my freedom rather than take it away. Glory, hallelujah! Amen.

---

1. Ellen G. White, *The Adventist Home* (Washington, DC: Review and Herald®, 1952), 117; emphasis added.

Chapter 8

Might Fakes Right

The Global Oppression of Women

In 1989, *New York Times* columnist Nicholas D. Kristof and reporter Sheryl WuDunn showed up at the Tiananmen Square massacre where military troops with assault rifles and tanks killed between four hundred and eight hundred unarmed civilians. "It was the human rights story of the year," they write in their book *Half the Sky: Turning Oppression Into Opportunity for Women Worldwide*.

Their story took an unexpected turn after Tiananmen. "The following year, we came across an obscure but meticulous demographic study that outlined a human rights violation that had claimed tens of thousands more lives. This study found that thirty-nine thousand baby girls die annually in China because parents don't give them the same medical care and attention that boys receive—and that is just in the first year of life."

The authors go on to describe how Chinese parents, because of their preference for male children, will quickly seek medical care for their boys but delay or neglect caring for the girls. "The result is that as many infant girls die unnecessarily *every week* in China as protesters died in the one incident at Tiananmen. Those Chinese girls never received a column inch of news coverage, and we began to wonder if our journalistic priorities were skewed."[1]

Every week a human-rights violation the size of the Tiananmen Square massacre is perpetrated on *infant girls*! It was a pivotal moment for Kristof and WuDunn.

The couple embarked on a life quest to improve the lives of women globally. They traveled extensively, acquainting themselves with a broad range of cultures, noticing similar patterns of devaluation of women in many of them. Not only did they chronicle the conditions they observed, but they also found microloan programs that helped women start small businesses.

They tell the story of Saima, who was poor and routinely beaten by her unemployed husband. She signed up with a Pakistani microfinance group called the Kashf Foundation to take out a sixty-five-dollar loan to buy beads and cloth for an embroidery business. She used the profits to buy more supplies, finally hiring helpers and ultimately her own husband! Because Kashf cared enough to give her a chance, Saima found better circumstances.[2] Kristof and WuDunn weave these stories throughout the book.

Being a postfeminism Westerner, I have had to endure only relatively mild versions of the oppression chronicled in *Half the Sky.* The fact is that we in the West are largely insulated from the horrors our sisters experience worldwide. As a believer in the Bible, I can't help seeing that the sad realities of the global oppression of women eerily fulfill Genesis

3:16—but in the most capricious, extreme way that bears the signature of the cosmic villain rather than the Hero. What follows is a brief overview of the three-part punishment and how it has been exploited as Satan has driven it outside God's intended boundaries.

Pain and toil in childbearing

Satan shows his hatred of life through global maternal mortality rates, which soar for want of basic medical care, especially in the developing world. More than three hundred thousand women die per year because of the complications of pregnancy and childbirth—about one every two minutes.[3] In the United States, maternal mortality rates soared during World War I—more women died in childbirth than men died in the war—but plunged between 1920 and 1940 when women obtained the right to vote.[4]

Education also factors in heavily. "The World Bank has estimated that for every one thousand girls who get one additional year of education, two fewer women will die in childbirth."[5] But of the world's 750 million illiterate adults, 63 percent are women.[6] Essentially, studies show a strong correlation between social marginalization and high maternal mortality.

If a woman can survive the birth process, she will face the sometimes overwhelming stress of caregiving in the family system. Research shows that a daughter or daughter-in-law is most likely to assume the role of caregiver in the absence of a spouse who can provide care. This is followed by a granddaughter and finally a son.[7] The burden of childcare generally falls upon women, as does the care of anyone in the family system who needs assistance. Like it or not, we are nurturers, and this costs us.

Your desire shall be for your husband

The devil digs the burden of caregiving in deeper by turning women into enablers, codependents, and doormats. Women's vulnerability in caring for the weak members of the family system can place us in positions of dependency best supported by a strong provider, but men don't always step up to the plate. Our desire to have such men as partners often leads us to project upon men virtues they don't possess.

We all know strong, competent women who, for some strange reason, stay in relationships with deadbeat guys. I would argue that this is part of the desire-for-your-husband phenomenon, which the enemy too often diverts to men who don't deserve the title *house-band*, for they do nothing to band the house together.

Even though competent, women often assume they are lacking. Imposter syndrome—defined as a psychological phenomenon in which knowledgeable individuals feel they will be unmasked as frauds—affects more women than men. We see a version of this in the fact that while 96 percent of US citizens say they would vote for a female president, US politics are still largely dominated by men. At all levels of government, women have performed as well as men, yet too few women run for political office to change it. Why? One poll found that "the women surveyed were less likely than the men to think they were qualified to run and serve and less likely to consider themselves competitive or confident."[8]

Women more often fall prey to anxiety and depression. Generalized anxiety disorder, panic disorder, and specific phobias all afflict women twice as often as men; depression is far more prevalent in women than in men.[9] Women have more dependent, avoidant, histrionic, and borderline personality disorders.[10] Perhaps because the female brain has lower levels of serotonin than the male brain,[11] women tend toward more fear and sadness and men toward anger and aggression. While girls' self-esteem peaks in childhood, it plummets after pubescence when we struggle with self-confidence related to both physical appearance and intellectual ability.[12] So often women place their low self-esteem at the mercy of men who treat them badly enough to drive it further down. My sisters, "an enemy hath done this" (Matthew 13:28, KJV)!

He shall rule over you

The serpent slithers into families and societies to put women at an unfair, and often dangerous, power disadvantage. One in three women worldwide have been raped, beaten, or coerced into sex in their lifetimes. On average, 30 percent of "women who have been in a relationship report that they have experienced some form of physical and/or sexual violence" by their partner. "Globally, as many as 38% of murders of women are committed by a male intimate partner."[13] The World Health Organization estimates that more than two hundred million women, mostly in Africa, endure the rite of female genital mutilation.[14]

Sadly, permission for wife and child beating often comes from the influence of fundamentalist religion. Many of the "countries where girls are cut, killed for honor, or kept out of school or the workplace typically have large Muslim populations." This may be politically incorrect to note, but it is factually correct.[15] In addition, Hinduism and Christianity have their own pockets of oppression as well. One study showed a correlation between fundamentalist Christianity and domestic violence approval; but no such correlation with moderate Christianity.[16]

A subtler violence is poverty. Women continue to join the work force in greater numbers but still earn 20 percent less than men globally.[17] While women are showing up more often in leadership, they still hold only about 16 percent of government positions worldwide.[18] This is tragic, since women would likely spend more wisely; female leaders tend to use more money for nutrition and education and less for alcohol and war.

In essence, authoritarianism, whether in Christianity, Islam, Hinduism, or another religion, results in violence against women. Some forms of fundamentalism call beating women and children "leading" in the home.

Subtler forms of undervaluing can be found in the "more advanced" Western culture. For instance, as film actresses age beyond their sexual prime in the United States, they tend to be "underrepresented, unattractive, unfriendly, and unintelligent" in films.[19] Generally, female actors earn less than male counterparts, and this earning power correlates more with youth and sex appeal.

In 2013, the median age of the most successful male actors was 46.5, while the female median age was 34.8. "Roughly a third of female speaking characters are shown in sexually revealing attire or are partially naked."[20] No wonder most women are dissatisfied with their bodies, and no wonder female self-esteem correlates strongly with appearance.[21]

The global oppression and undervaluing of women begs the question, Did God assign all this for eating a piece of fruit? No matter how disobedient Eve was, no merciful and good God would prescribe these horrifying afflictions for a sin committed within a few moments' time. God is not the Author of unending torture and unlimited retribution. He doesn't roast people in hellfire for the sins of one lifetime or even put them in unending hell on earth for the sins of one moment.

As I established earlier, God designed Eve's punishment to be carried out in the context of a family led by a servant-leader. In that context, the curse would become a blessing as the marriage institution became a means of symbolizing and demonstrating the relationship between Christ and His bride. In this way and many others, God's punishment for sin would be redemptive rather than destructive. But as we view the lot of women worldwide, we see ruin everywhere. What happened?

An enemy hath done this

When God turned the curse into a blessing, the enemy of God turned it back into a curse.

God said,

> "I will greatly multiply your sorrow and your
>   conception;
> In pain you shall bring forth children;
> Your desire shall be for your husband,
> And he shall rule over you" (Genesis 3:16).

The enemy said, "I will greatly multiply your pain, exhaustion, and difficulty in bearing alone, without help, the burdens of the young, the old, the disabled, and also many adults who could take care of themselves but won't. In pain, you shall bring forth all these real and pseudochildren, in

81

many cases without a husband or help from anyone else. Yet you will possess an innate craving for approval and affection; a craving that I will constantly excite toward ungodly and unworthy people—mostly men. Many of these unworthy, selfish ones will deprive and even abuse you. They shall rule over you, unfairly and oppressively dominating you physically, emotionally, socially, politically, and financially."

Women the world over suffer because Satan has rerouted the consequences of sin to be far more disastrous than God intended. This is a bad thing—a very bad thing.

But it isn't the *last* thing. The enemy has forgotten that God delights in turning curses, even secondhand curses, into blessings. God will have the last word. That last Word is Jesus, and He gives "beauty for ashes" and pours healing ointment over all our sufferings (Isaiah 61:3). The disciple who understood this best, and who poured back the most famous ointment in history, was a woman.

Journaling

As you contemplate the experiences of women the world over, what is your deepest desire for womankind?

_____

_____

_____

_____

_____

_____

Prayer

Dear grieving God,

As I see Your pain at the affliction of womankind, I see Your love. You hate how the enemy has twisted Your words and makes You seem more like a heartless tyrant than a self-giving God. Help me to separate the enemy's lies about You from the truth so that I can always keep You, the God who is love, at the center of my heart. Amen.

---

1. Nicholas D. Kristof and Sheryl WuDunn, *Half the Sky: Turning Oppression Into Opportunity for Women Worldwide* (New York: Vintage Books, 2010), xiv.

2. Kristof and WuDunn, *Half the Sky*, 184–187.

3. World Health Organization, "Maternal Mortality," fact sheet, last updated November 2016, http://www.who.int/mediacentre/factsheets/fs348/en/.

4. Kristof and WuDunn, *Half the Sky*, 116.

5. Kristof and WuDunn, *Half the Sky*, 114.

6. UNESCO Institute for Statistics, "Literacy Rates Continue to Rise From One Generation to the Next," Fact Sheet no. 45, September 2017, http://uis.unesco.org/sites/default/files/documents/fs45-literacy-rates-continue-rise-generation-to-next-en-2017_0.pdf.

7. Administration on Aging.

8. Karlyn Bowman and Jennifer K. Marsico, "The Past, Present, and Future of the Women's Vote," American Enterprise Institute, October 4, 2012, http://www.aei.org/publication/the-past-present-and-future-of-the-womens-vote/.

9. Anxiety and Depression Association of America, "Facts and Statistics," news release, last modified August 2017, http://www.adaa.org/about-adaa/press-room/facts-statistics. See also "Depression," Centers for Disease Control and Prevention, last modified October 4, 2013, http://www.cdc.gov/mentalhealth/data_stats/depression.htm.

10. Andre Venter, "Personality Disorder Statistics—Out of the Fog," *Psychology Blog*, May 5, 2017, http://psycheblog.uk/2017/05/05/personality-disorder-statistics-out-of-the-fog-2/. See the chart "UK 2009–2010 Personality Disorder Hospital Admissions by Gender" for specifics.

11. "Sex Differences in the Brain's Serotonin System," Science Daily, February 17, 2008, https://www.sciencedaily.com/releases/2008/02/080213111043.htm.

12. Suzanne Daley, "Little Girls Lose Their Self-Esteem Way to Adolescence,

Study Finds," *New York Times*, January 9, 1991, http://www.nytimes.com /1991/01/09/education/little-girls-lose-their-self-esteem-way-to-adolescence -study-finds.html.

13. World Health Organization, "Violence Against Women," fact sheet, last modified November 2017, http://www.who.int/mediacentre/factsheets/fs239/en/.

14. "Sexual and Reproductive Health: Female Genital Mutilation (FGM)," World Health Organization, accessed November 30, 2017, http://www.who.int /reproductivehealth/topics/fgm/prevalence/en/.

15. Kristof and WuDunn, *Half the Sky*, 149.

16. Jerome Koch and Ignacio Ramirez, "Religiosity, Christian Fundamentalism, and Intimate Partner Violence Among U.S. College Students," *Review of Religious Research* 51, no. 4 (2010): 401–410.

17. "Inequality in Employment," UNICEF, accessed November 30, 2017, http://www.unicef.org/sowc07/profiles/inequality_employment.php.

18. Martha Chen, Joann Vanek, Francie Lund, James Heintz with Renana Jhabvala, and Christine Bonner, *Progress of the World's Women 2005: Women, Work, and Poverty* (New York: United Nations Development Fund for Women, 2005), 8, http://www.un-ngls.org/orf/women-2005.pdf.

19. Doris G. Bazzini, William D. McIntosh, Stephen M. Smith, Sabrina Cook, and Caleigh Harris, "The Aging Woman in Popular Film: Underrepresented, Unattractive, Unfriendly, and Unintelligent," *Sex Roles: A Journal of Research* 36, no. 7–8 (April 1997): 531–543.

20. "Gender Inequality in Film: In Infographic Form," IndieWire, November 28, 2013, http://www.indiewire.com/article/gender-inequality-film-in-infographic -form.

21. Kate Fox, "Mirror, Mirror: A Summary of Research Findings on Body Image," Social Issues Research Centre, accessed November 30, 2017, http://www.sirc .org/publik/mirror.html.

Chapter 9

Follow the Spikenard Trail

How God Can Turn Oppression Into Opportunity

I'm writing this book because I lost my voice.

As a teen, I discovered I could sing and then sometime later that I could write songs. As a new singer-songwriter, I felt I had discovered my life purpose. Tragically, only ten years into what I hoped would be a lifelong career path, I began to have health-related vocal problems. Although I kept singing for many years, I never did so with ease or confidence, and I knew my ability to use my voice would be limited.

Out of the rubble of my disappointment, I searched for a new sense of purpose. God led me to write. Since I was always bound by rhyme and meter, writing prose felt like an exhilarating free fall. I went from articles to Bible studies to authoring books; now I write all day just as I used to sing all day. It is as if the vessel of my voice broke to release another gift I would never have discovered otherwise.

Brokenness is good. It is not good because suffering,

85

sickness, oppression, abuse, injustice, and all the myriad mutations of sin are good. Clearly, "an enemy hath done this" (Matthew 13:28, KJV); but brokenness is good because of what God creates with the things the enemy does.

God's perfect will was a sinless universe. His redemptive will is a universe saved from sin, which ultimately brings about His perfect will. His love pours through the cracks of His broken purpose more fully than if it had never broken.

Jesus, in His life on earth, strove to communicate this gospel—this good news of how God can shine through brokenness. He chose the cross; a place where heavy spikes could fracture bones, blood vessels, and cartilage, and where His own soul shattered to pieces beneath the tonnage of the world's sin. This was the stage from which He would make His greatest proclamation of the paradoxical power of weakness.

Nevertheless, even after the Cross revealed to the onlooking universe the unstoppable love of God against the unspeakable evil of His enemy, "the principles at stake were to be more fully revealed."[1] Not just angels, but humans still needed to be convinced of the truth about God.

It is easy for us, with our sinful history and the sheer momentum of sin and its consequences in our lives, to assume that a sinless God can't empathize with us. *How can He know what it is like to fail again and again when He never failed?* While we err in our conclusions, God is big enough to find a way past our defenses. He did so very creatively in raising up Mary Magdalene, a sinner (and a woman!), to reflect His generosity and compassion so completely that He Himself would in effect point to her and say, "Look at her, and you will see My cross. Wherever this gospel is preached, tell what she's done."

What is the *gospel*? His life, death, and resurrection; in other words, His story. This means that in essence Jesus said, "Wherever you tell My story, tell her story." His story will be told "in all the world . . . , and then the end will come" (Matthew 24:14). Before time comes to a close, every living, breathing, volitional being will have heard Jesus' story. They will also have heard the story of Mary Magdalene.

Mary Magdalene, a demon-possessed, mentally ill woman; Mary Magdalene, a victim of sexual abuse, incest, and clergy abuse who *became* a demon-possessed, mentally ill woman, and likely a prostitute, because of these things. Is there anything more broken than a sufferer of such inhumanity who acts out, thus deepening the wound, adding sin to sin and finally ending up socially scorned, compulsively addicted, psychologically compromised, and inhabited by devils?

No, nothing is more broken. But in God's hands, broken is good.

Mary's fall embodies the enemy's plan to destroy women. He does so through the things we have identified as women's particular weak points: codependency and approval addiction, which place us under the power of ungodly, exploitative people. The enemy takes the threefold curse—(1) pain and toil in childbearing; (2) your desire shall be for your husband; and (3) he shall rule over you—outside the bounds of a godly, servant-leader-led marriage and into his jungle where the love of power displaces the power of love. There we acquire the majority of our wounds, and there Mary Magdalene did too.

Mary's parents never appear in the gospel story. We don't know why. But apparently a relative, Simon the Pharisee, stepped into that vacancy to mentor the young woman. Being a Pharisee, Simon exalted the Law even as he remained a stranger to grace. The result was an unconverted heart masquerading as a standard-bearing champion of righteousness. Where would Simon go with his lust, his pride, and his need for selfish pleasure? He would have to hide it from the eyes of his enamored public. In the darkness of secret sin, he lived a double life.

Many a Pharisee took advantage of vulnerable women; the story of the woman taken in adultery provides a case in point. The unnamed woman mentioned in John 8:1–11 lived in Jerusalem. One day a group of scribes and Pharisees set up a sting operation; they snatched the woman naked from the trap they had laid, brought her before Jesus, and implored, "Teacher, this woman was caught in adultery, in the very act. Now Moses, in the law, commanded us that such should be stoned. But what do You say?"

He said, "He who is without sin among you," meaning the sin of sexual immorality, "let him throw a stone at her first" (John 8:4, 5, 7). When He again proceeded to document their crimes in the dirt, they faded away one by one—hoping to void the exposure of their secret sins.

Sexual misconduct was rampant among the Pharisees in Jesus' day. It is rampant among Pharisees today. It presents possibly the most damaging form of sexual abuse because the clergy serve as God's representatives, and the violation of trust destroys trust in God. Because it signals the toxicity of an entire family system, incest correlates with much more psychological damage than nonincestuous abuse. But I would argue that clergy abuse is at least as damaging because it is spiritual incest, in which the fathers and mothers in Israel exploit, rather than protect, the weaker members of the family.

The perpetrators standing there beside the fallen woman skulked away into the darkness, leaving her alone with the only One who could heal her. And heal her He did, just as He healed Mary Magdalene.

We don't know just how Mary's healing took place, but we do know that her gratitude led her to spend her life savings on a bottle of perfume.

"Sir, I would like the finest you have," she announced to the apothecary owner one day. Jesus had said three times He would die, and one of those times He specified that He would be crucified (Mark 8:31–33; Matthew 16:21–23; 20:17–19).

Troubled by this news, Mary nevertheless determined that He should have a proper burial and purposed in her heart to buy burial ointment fit for a king. The double benefit of this would be that she would get around the old Levitical law that said, "You must not bring the earnings of a female prostitute . . . to pay any vow" (Deuteronomy 23:18). By purchasing burial ointment, Mary would be giving to Jesus while avoiding disobedience to Moses.

Mary was like an old towel. New towels have fabric softeners and unbroken fibers that render them very fluffy and pretty but rather poor at absorbing water. Throw those new towels into the wash with harsh detergents, tennis shoes, and bleach, then tumble them around in the hot dryer with the shoes and other clothes, repeating the process twenty or thirty times, and you have an old, thirsty towel that can absorb the water off your skin from about five feet away.

When Jesus said, "I am going to die," and the disciples ignored it, Mary drank it in. She believed Him. She absorbed what He said. She was an old towel. This led her to the apothecary shop that day with a little bag full of her life savings folded into her robes.

You can't afford the best I have, the shop owner thought, eyeing the humble dress of a disciple of Jesus. He went back to his storeroom to get a bargain bottle, emerging in fine form, wafting it before her nose.

"Nice. How much?" she asked.

"Fifty dollars," he said.

"Sir, I want your finest."

Persistent woman, he thought, fetching a hundred-dollar bottle. The exchange rolled out similarly, with Mary insisting she could afford his finest perfume.

"You don't look like you can afford it," he said. "You look like a farmer's wife. The finest I have is for royalty."

"I want it," she insisted.

What is it about her? She's so believable. The man at last crawled up the ladder that led to his private room and fished an alabaster box from a chest under his bed. Crawling down, he placed the box on the counter—a beacon gleaming in the hot Near Eastern sun.

"Ma'am, *this* is the finest I have. It is an alabaster box filled with spikenard, the *Nardostachys jatamansi* flower, harvested from the death-defying heights of the Himalaya Mountains. I can't let you sample its fragrance, ma'am, because once this box is broken, it can never be resealed. All the ointment will come pouring forth when it breaks. It is meant to be used as an extravagant display of affection and even worship for a great king."

"I will take it."

"Do you have thirty-five thousand dollars?"[2]

The afternoon was silent for a time until the woman reached into the folds of her robe and began to count out silver coins. The shop owner blinked in disbelief, the silver radiating wealth on the walls of his shop. At last, every cent of the asking price lay before him. He wrapped the box in a small silk cloth and handed it to the woman, who tucked it away in a place very near her pounding, grateful heart.

She bought it for His burial, but a rumor began to circulate that Jesus would be crowned King of Israel! *Our bondage will soon be over!* Could it be? The hope brought ecstasy powerful enough to push Mary through her fear of public scorn. Simon would be hosting a party; although she would not be welcome, she would be tolerated as a relative. She set out on her joyful expedition to honor Jesus as King.

Arriving, she saw Him.

Jesus. He had saved her from the torment of demons. He had freed her from hell's chokehold. She knew, just knew, He was God's Messiah. She broke the box, and her heart broke along with it. The tears poured down as she flung herself at His feet; hands cupping the rich ointment and pouring it out on His beautiful head, hands, and feet.

She lost herself in worship.

She had hoped no one would notice, but she had forgotten the power of the fragrance. It rose up from her hands and took possession of the room, forcing the guests to look for its source, which they found in the weeping woman surrounded by alabaster shards. They knew the smell of money. They knew instantly she had spent a fortune on this weak, silly act of extravagance. And they scorned her without restraint.

Then Jesus stepped in. He said two things essentially: "Stop it" and "God is using her." "Why do you trouble the

91

woman?" He said, "Wherever this gospel is preached in the whole world, what this woman has done will also be told as a memorial to her" (Matthew 26:10, 13).

Jesus wants the abusers, oppressors, and silencers of women to stop it. He also wants our stories of healing to be told all over the world.

The enemy of womankind, the devil, abuses us through those who devalue our half of God's creation. Jesus says to them, "Leave her alone." But He also promises, through the experience of Mary Magdalene and countless other redeemed among womankind, that He can use our stories of brokenness and that He can pour through the cracks of our futile existence like spikenard, making the air fragrant with the love of the Divine Recycler.

Apart from her conscious notice, moved by the Spirit, Mary created a portrait of the Cross. She filled the air with fragrance, just as Jesus filled the cosmos with a "sweetsmelling savour" (Ephesians 5:2, KJV). She "wasted" her treasure, as Jesus "wasted" His blood on millions who would never yield to its power. She stood in the midst of scorn, just as Jesus, even while He shed the blood that gave them breath, heard His blood-bought children use that breath to curse Him.

A week after Simon's feast, the sweat from the Crucifixion exhumed the last of the spikenard from Jesus' pores. Hanging there, disoriented, traumatized, and broken, He may have smelled the fragrance and remembered the love of one who "got" Him, who absorbed His love, and then poured it back.

Make sure that whatever your pain, whatever your losses, whatever your complicated mess, your life is soaked in the love of Jesus and then poured out again.

Journaling

How does the story of Mary intersect with your story? Are there any similarities?

_____

_____

_____

_____

_____

_____

_____

_____

Prayer

Broken and spilled-out God,

You poured Yourself out till nothing, not even life itself, remained. Now I want to pour myself out for You. Make me like Mary, who allowed the Holy Spirit to move through her so freely that she lost all self-consciousness in her offering of precious ointment. I want my offering to comfort You in Your sorrow. I want my life to reflect Yours. Pour through Me, Jesus. Amen.

_____

1. White, *The Desire of Ages*, 761.

2. The monetary amounts have been adjusted to dollars for this story; but in Jesus' time, a working man's wage was a denarius a day (Matthew 20:13) and the perfume could have been sold for three hundred denarii (John 12:5).

Chapter 10

The Tale of Two Sisters

The Why and How of Self-Care

*I*t is a well-known tale of two sisters. The first sister over-extends herself and burns out; the second sister works hard, too, but takes time to recharge, ultimately proving herself more resourceful than the first sister. Could it be that God gives the tale of Mary and Martha wide exposure to teach us something? Could it be that among other things they demonstrate the blessings of self-care?

Martha worked so hard. She also carried a lot of guilt—enough to share some with her sister, Mary, who didn't work quite as hard. Jesus diagnosed Martha with generalized anxiety disorder: "You are worried and troubled about many things," He said. Mary, on the other hand, took time to recharge, choosing "that good part" (Luke 10:41, 42). She knew that the only thing that stood between her and demon possession was time with Jesus, and so she made time (verses 38–42).

Martha's reputation as a resourceful, dedicated community

and church pillar surrounded her like a cloud of applause. People had a harder time placing Mary; they were not sure what to think of her sketchy past. *Uh, she's kind of . . . frail. She will probably never amount to much, but God loves all kinds.*

Then a crisis hit: an arrest, a trial, and a crucifixion. They all forsook Jesus and fled, except perhaps the women—and Mary Magdalene, who watched every cruel abuse as her heart bled with love (Matthew 27:55, 56). Then they laid Jesus' cold, limp body in a grave behind a big stone that seemed like a giant, cruel period at the end of the sentence: "Your Messiah is dead."

At dawn on Sunday, several women visited that grave with anointing spices, only to find His body gone. In the drama that ensued, the risen Jesus honored one woman by appearing first to her. She took the message "He's alive!" and became the first to preach a resurrected Jesus (John 20:1–18).

Mary Magdalene supported Jesus in the crisis of His trial and crucifixion. Mary Magdalene couldn't keep herself away, even from His grave, and as a result saw Him alive and carried that torch of hope to the disciples in crisis. Mary came through as a true heroine in a time of need. But where was Martha? There is no mention of her in those moments. This is like the often-told story of the tortoise and the hare—the Energizer Bunny. The simple fact is that the one who recharges lasts the longest and ultimately serves the best.

Spiritual renewal
Let us realize something rather than throw our hands up

and say, "It's inevitable! God said it would happen, and it is happening!" Something that stands between us and the inevitable. This something is big; it is profound; it is life altering; and it is so obvious that we miss it. Ready?

We have choices. We can choose to resist our tendencies to overextend to the point of exhaustion. We can rethink our compulsion to help when it actually hurts. We can choose to live in a rational manner, preserving our strength so that we have something to pour out when the time comes. Remember, Mary had to save up her money to be able to buy the spikenard.

We can learn self-care. What? Isn't self-care right up there with selfishness, self-indulgence, self-centeredness, and self-exaltation? Many of us read the biblical counsel to put others before ourselves and assume that *any* self-concern is malignantly sinful. For instance, "Do nothing out of selfish ambition or vain conceit. Rather, in humility *value others above yourselves*, not looking to your own interests but each of you to the interests of the others" (Philippians 2:3, 4, NIV; emphasis added).

The Bible seems to reject self-valuing categorically. Those of us with tender consciences sometimes apply this too indiscriminately, expending ourselves until we resemble a dried-up Brillo Pad. Then one day we react: You know what? No more of this! I am going to be selfish for a change!

But God *does* call us to unselfish service. All of heaven is characterized by the spirit of service and an utter, ecstatic self-abandonment. Nature thrives because one unit continually gives to another, which then gives to another, and so on down the line of generosity. God is self-giving love, and He made us in His image. So how do we live like Jesus and give

Damsel, Arise!

like Jesus without ending up in the Brillo Pad graveyard?

It all boils down to motive. I can care for myself selfishly, or I can care for myself unselfishly. When I care for myself selfishly, I am a stagnant pond, holding on to my water only to have it putrefy with algae overgrowth. When I care for myself unselfishly, I am a river pooling for a time, only to build up enough water to spill forth in rich, life-giving currents.

Self-centeredness works against our very design. As self-preservation morphs into self-destruction, we become confused and disoriented. Like the belly of a glutton, the consequences of our narcissism eventually balloon into reality. When we live to serve God and others, we may at times look selfish as we collect our energies and gather our resources, but in fact we will be serving God just as verily as when we are pouring them out.

Over the long haul, we will take more than we give if we fail at self-care. Many a do-gooder burns out to a bitter, grumpy pile of ashes and is a burden to everyone around. Health problems may sap them of strength, or unmanaged anxiety and/or depression may paralyze them.

Out of a certain helplessness, some of us recoil at the idea of self-care. Like children, we want someone else to care for us. Unfortunately, this desire is only realistic until we are about eighteen years old. Generous, busy, caregiving women long for someone to care for *them* for a change. When that someone never appears, we feel alone and unloved.

As a sister in this suffering, I propose a simple solution: Let us mother ourselves—but on God's behalf. Let us be the hands and feet of God to ourselves as we decide to soak in a hot tub, take the time to make a healthy meal, or take the afternoon off for a long walk in our favorite forest. Make these choices as God's representative to yourself. He loves you! He longs to pull you to Himself in tender affection, meeting your every need and desire. So do it for Him.

"We are therefore Christ's ambassadors, as though God were making his appeal through us. We implore you on Christ's behalf: Be reconciled to God" (2 Corinthians 5:20, NIV). Sister, *you* are a child of God! Represent His love to yourself.

So many women deprive or even harm themselves in ways they would never think of inflicting upon others. Often the reasoning is that they own themselves and they declare themselves to be worthless, so they can do as they wish. Seriously? Listen to yourselves! What saith the Lord? "Do you not know . . . you are not your own? For you were bought at a price; therefore glorify God in your body and in your spirit, which are God's" (1 Corinthians 6:19, 20). God requires you to treat yourself with respect because you are His child. You do beautifully in applying this to other people. Now apply it to *yourself.*

How do we define *self-care*? The simplest explanation I know is this: *Self-care* is rejuvenation through doing something that you enjoy that is also good for you. You may like ice cream, but it is not good for you. Going to the dentist is good for you, but you probably don't like it. It is *like* and *healthy* together that create the synergy.

My self-care list is simple: I read memoirs, bike, hike, cook good food, reach out to friends and loved ones, take baths, teach my dog tricks, play guitar, and dance (in my living room—it is great exercise). I also pray in such a way that it releases stress as opposed to adding more stress: I cry to Jesus, tears streaming down; I tell Him exactly what I think and feel, not fearing judgment; and I process issues just as I process with a good friend. This kind of prayer can powerfully rejuvenate.

Make your own self-care list, and learn how to use it!

If we don't care for ourselves, chances are we will self-indulge. Think of the overworked nurse strung out on Percocet or the mother self-consigned to the slavery of elaborate meals, grazing herself into obesity. These women deprive themselves, failing to obtain the rest they need, then self-indulge out of sheer exhaustion.

Often the "licensing effect" fuels the process. As two professors put it, "A prior choice, which activates and boosts a positive self-concept, subsequently licenses the choice of a more self-indulgent option."[1] In other words, the martyr syndrome of overwork, overgiving, and self-deprivation makes us feel entitled to a few pills or cookies or temper tantrums, or—you complete the list. To care for ourselves in a reasonable way, besides preserving our health, confronts and slays the martyr within.

As you begin this process of taking responsibility for your own health and well-being, those who have accustomed themselves to your overburdened ways may rebel, criticize, and feel abandoned. Patiently explain the change you are making in your life. Take responsibility for the excesses of the past, and admit you may shoot too far the other way. Solicit their help for your recovery; their anger just might melt into compassion. If not, you have the Word of God on your side, for He says, "Present your bodies a living sacrifice, holy, acceptable to God, which is your reasonable service [of worship]" (Romans 12:1). Stand in His strength alone, and take the rest of the day off to do it.

Journaling

Write out your self-care list. In other words, what self-rejuvenating things do you like that are also good for you?

_____

_____

_____

_____

_____

_____

_____

Prayer

Dear health-guardian God,

Wow, I feel safer with You just knowing that You actually want me to feel good. Help me out of the ditch of self-deprivation, but then keep me from falling into the ditch of self-indulgence. As I learn to care appropriately for my physical, mental, and spiritual health, make me an example to other women who need healing. Help me just to be grateful for life; taking breaks from always needing to accomplish something. Help me to rest in Your unfailing love and righteousness. Amen.

---

1. Uzma Khan and Ravi Dhar, "Licensing Effect in Consumer Choice," abstract, *Journal of Marketing Research* 43, no. 2 (May 2006): 259–266.

Chapter 11

Women and Self-Worth

The Good Way to Feel Good About Yourself

An American tourist purchased an inexpensive amber necklace in a Parisian trinket shop. After he was asked for a large sum to pay the customs duties in New York, the man became curious and had the necklace appraised. "I will give you twenty-five thousand dollars for it," the jeweler said. Now even more curious, the man took it to another jeweler who offered thirty-five thousand dollars.

"What is so valuable about this necklace?" the man finally asked.

"Look through this glass," the jeweler said. The man squinted through the jeweler's magnifying glass to see the writing: "From Napoleon Bonaparte to Josephine."

Association with fame increases value.

Did it ever occur to us that we are associated with the Monarch of the universe? And that He has established our value beyond any appraisal? The question at issue now is whether we value ourselves.

One of the results of Eve's sin was a certain desire toward her husband. As I have tried to show, God's design was that this desire be expressed toward a servant-leader, who would highly esteem and appreciate his wife, leading her to feel safe and satisfied in his presence. All men fall short of this sometimes, and some fall short of it all the time. Ultimately, we must look to Jesus, the never-failing Servant-Leader of all women, who values us infinitely.

Listen to these probing words from a woman of experience: "The Lord is disappointed when His people place a low estimate upon themselves. He desires His chosen heritage to value themselves according to the price He has placed upon them."[1] My paraphrase of this wise counsel would be that God's heart sinks when we have low self-esteem. He wants us to value ourselves infinitely. He wants us not just to accept His valuation of us, but to esteem *ourselves* according to the infinite price of His own life, which sustains everything in the cosmos.

We humans are unusual creatures. We have much higher levels of self-awareness than the other animals in creation, from dogs and cats to star-nosed moles and hairy frogfish. My Chihuahua barks maniacally at larger dogs; she has no idea how small she is. By way of contrast, I am far too self-conscious to bark at large dogs or even yell at large people. Humans' self-concepts develop out of a mysterious blend of social comparison and a cerebrally mediated capacity to self-reflect. At any rate, we *Homo sapiens* will, by virtue of our very nature, have some kind of self-image. It might as well be a good one.

The world answers this need by promoting self-esteem as a panacea for all of life's psychological ills. But science itself disproves the consistency of its value. While high self-esteem does increase social confidence, it doesn't seem to prevent risky behaviors, such as promiscuity or substance abuse in teens. It also doesn't appear to increase a person's popularity, work, or academic performance. In fact, people with high self-esteem tend to sever relationships when they become conflicted, and perpetrators of domestic violence often have high self-esteem.[2] The Bible condemns pride for a reason; it reduces the quality of our characters even as prideful individuals esteem themselves to have superior qualities.

Low self-esteem isn't the answer either. Some of us like to belittle ourselves in an attempt to stay humble. While self-effacing behavior has its place, we must guard against false humility. For many years, I would respond to compliments with self put-downs. One day the Holy Spirit revealed my true motives: I was actually trying to protect myself against other people humiliating me by putting myself down first. When I invalidated people's sincere affirmations, I actually insulted them; but I was too caged in my own self-protective trap to notice.

We tend to anchor our self-worth in transient things: our beauty, our abilities, our accomplishments, our money, or our social standing, to name a few examples. These things enhance our self-worth based on how we measure up against other people. This means that even if one day you feel pretty, capable, accomplished, wealthy, and well liked, another person who exceeds you in these things can cause your fragile self-worth to crash. Realistically, our beauty and abilities will fade; our accomplishments will be outdone; our money will be spent; and our social standing will shift throughout life until on our deathbed only our loved ones surround us.

Putting our self-worth in what we are, what we have, or what we can do sets us up for disappointment. On the other hand, basing our self-worth on the price Jesus paid for us creates an unshakable soul foundation. From that solid footing, we can authenticate His valuation of us by being of value to other human beings. His downward-falling blessing upon our heads can be channeled horizontally through our outstretched hands as we find our place in this world. Each person has been uniquely gifted by God; you can do one thing no one else can do, and that is be yourself. When we seek, not pride, but purpose, we find a little corner, however small and humble, to brighten with His light shining through our unique prism. In Jesus, we seek to *bless*, not to *best*, other people.

Research has shown repeatedly that women overall have lower self-esteem than men. Instead of having a little pity party for all of us, let me be frank. Low self-esteem is inverted pride. We may not feel superior, but we would like to. Most of us with low self-esteem have a terrible habit of comparing ourselves with others. Listen to Paul: "For we dare not class ourselves or compare ourselves with those who commend themselves. But they, measuring themselves by themselves, and comparing themselves among themselves, are not wise" (2 Corinthians 10:12).

Comparing ourselves with others is *not wise*. I see this in myself and in the people I try to help. Comparison and competition lead to either inflated or devastated self-esteem.

In the competitive mind, we put people in one of two places—superior or inferior. Those of us with low self-esteem, like most women, feel inferior. But the fact is that we covet the place of superiority, operating from the same flawed foundation of comparison-based self-worth.

I find that those of us with low self-esteem tend to engage in deprecating self-talk, such as "I'm fat! I'm stupid! I'm ugly!" I call it emotional cutting because, like physical cutting, we seek to release tension that way. Physical injury releases endorphins, which explains why cutting can become addictive. I believe emotional cutting brings about a similar brain response, making us feel a certain momentary release of tension, only to reap a whirlwind of damage later. When I discover my counseling clients are engaging in this kind of behavior, I forbid it, and we work hard to find replacement scripts. And I forbid it in myself as well!

What if I told you that God had mapped out a way you could be so settled in your sense of value that you would reflexively share the Source with everyone around you? The way is simple. It is to become a new creature in Christ. "If any woman is in Christ, she is a new creature. Old things have passed away; behold, new things have come" (2 Corinthians 5:17, my paraphrase).

Don't fear that in following Jesus you will lose your individuality; Jesus died for the freedom that gives our individuality to us. We can see this in the fact that in prophecy God symbolizes coercive, controlling religion as a *beast*. He hates anything that compromises individual conscience and character. Why would Jesus die for your individuality, then obliterate it when you choose to follow Him? Far from it! When you give Him your will, He gives it back to you, refined, purified, and strengthened.

When you become a new creature, you inherit a storehouse of blessings in Christ. You may not see all these things in yourself, but God sees them in you, for He sees the future of who you will become. Because God sees the future as clearly as the present, He doesn't become distracted by your deficiencies and failures as you do. Look through His heavenly lens at your future, and all your self-consciousness will melt away.

Just about the time your God-envisioned confidence rises to an optimal level, He will start giving you opportunities to engage in what doesn't generally come easily to many women—assertiveness. In the next chapter, we will look at how to assert oneself in such a way as to respect both ourselves and others and ensure the best outcome.

Journaling
How does it feel to know that God wants you to value yourself as of infinite worth?

_____

_____

_____

_____

_____

_____

_____

_____

_____

Prayer

Dear Infinite Giver,

I have failed to value myself the way You have valued me, and I have disappointed You in this. Lead me in a path that reflects Your will that I esteem myself according to the price You placed upon me when You poured out Your life on a lonely cross. Let that grateful self-valuation protect me from its counterfeits of pride and low self-esteem. Teach me how to stay true to this sense of value even when the world tries to tear me away. Thank You, Lord. Amen.

---

1. White, *The Desire of Ages*, 668.

2. Roy F. Baumeister, Jennifer D. Campbell, Joachim I. Krueger, and Kathleen D. Vohs, "Exploding the Self-Esteem Myth," *Scientific American* 292, no. 1 (January 2005): 84–91.

Chapter 12

Gracious Assertiveness

Look Up, Stand Up, Speak Up

I distinctly remember sitting with Pastor Zachary* and his charming wife for an after-church dinner while the pastor talked animatedly, almost without stopping to breathe. Wanting to think well of my host, I assumed that his verbosity was fueled by his passion for the subject matter. Pastor Zachary had discovered what he thought was a unique theological idea and had taken it upon himself to be a crusader for the cause of convincing everyone within his circle of its importance. The problem was that the circle was feeling a little uncomfortable, and what started out as warm embrace was now morphing into a boa constrictor's "hug."

Mrs. Zachary seemed the picture-perfect wife, cheerfully agreeing with her husband's ideas and obeying his rather abrupt commands. "Bring out the dessert now, dear," he said at one point, and "bring us some hot tea" at another. I began to feel party to the crime of bossing her around like

_____
* A pseudonym.

a maid and tried to show little tokens of respect, thinking I could salvage the situation. Then he went over the edge.

"The tea is too hot. Take it back into the kitchen until it cools down."

No "please," no "I'm sorry to bother you," no "Honey, you are so good to me." Nothing like that. Just bark out an order, and expect the obedient wife to comply.

I thought, *This woman is headed for a total collapse.*

I saw a hint of the collapse to come when Mr. Zachary said, "Dear, the baby has messed his pants. Take him away and change him."

Mrs. Zachary's face fell for the first time since I had arrived. The twinkly eyes turned dull, and the pretty curved lips flattened into a thin line.

"You." That is all she said, but the rage smoldered like lava beneath the crust of her pretty face. At that instant, I knew their marriage would never last.

Only a year or so later, I heard Mrs. Zachary had purposely had an affair just so her husband would divorce her. She wanted out so badly that she chose to bear the public shame of adultery rather than live with a boa constrictor. In such cases, I wonder who committed adultery first—Mrs. Zachary who loved another man, or Mr. Zachary who loved himself. At any rate, Mrs. Zachary's silent acceptance of his abuse did not serve her well. Although I don't know what happened behind the scenes, I wonder if more assertiveness on Mrs. Zachary's part could have provided Mr. Zachary with a needed wake-up call. Of course, I don't want to engage in victim blaming, but to a degree we do teach people how to treat us.

Often we so desire the approval of those around us that

we engage in appeasement behaviors to keep the peace. Since dominance and appeasement create an unhealthy power imbalance, we feel a sense of dissonance even while we placate. Sooner or later we will explode in anger, or we will implode in self-destruction at this unfair and unbalanced state.

Victims frequently are told they have no rights. The element of truth in this lie is what gives it power. The sinner's only "right to . . . enter through the gates" into God's presence is in Jesus Christ (Revelation 22:14). Our sins have forfeited our right to life itself, in such a way that all we truly deserve is our graves. This gospel truth rings deep in the heart of every sinner who knows her total unworthiness. All that comes from God is a gift; we have no rights before Him, except the rights He gives us.

As for our relationship with other human beings, now that is a different story. We do indeed have God-given rights before one another. This means we can require others to treat us fairly, decently, and respectfully. In order to paralyze us with guilt, master manipulators will sometimes co-opt the truth that we have no rights before God and generalize it to the human realm. I have heard many stories of abusers quoting Bible verses about unworthiness in order to make their victims feel undeserving of humane treatment. This is evil.

Even Jesus protected His rights. He escaped from stoning, from arrest, and from being thrown over a cliff (John 8:59; 10:39; Luke 4:28–30). The Scriptures are clear that He "gave Himself" to the cross and all the abuses therein for the purpose of saving us (Galatians 1:4; 1 Timothy 2:6). He submitted to abuse for the sake of the greater good, but

His toleration of it lends absolutely no virtue to the victimization itself.

When we submit ourselves to unnecessary abuse, we hurt not only ourselves but also the perpetrator. An enabler will sometimes carry a certain prideful contempt deep within because, after all, she has been a great Christian by allowing her rights to be violated and her needs ignored. She feels she must suffer "for Christ's sake." Codependent people in relationships with addicts are considered by addiction specialists to be coaddicted because they cooperate with the addict in living a lie.[1] False humility dishonors God and feeds unhealthy relationship systems.

If you or someone you love is suffering from abuse, realize that people are ready to help.[2] An abuser isolates his victim, making her feel as if no one will care if she cries out. Pray that God lifts the veil as He did for Elisha's servant, who saw horses and chariots of fire ready to protect God's people (2 Kings 6:17).

Fortunately, mistreatment doesn't go that far for most of us. While we may not be abused, we may feel invisible, taken for granted, or disrespected. We want to stop being so accommodating and actually "show up" for the relationship. Saying "I'm going to be more assertive . . . if that's OK with you" won't cut it. Hiding our true selves in order to be liked seems safe until we realize that the person they like isn't us at all but an avatar we project from a safe distance.

To experience love, we must be willing to share our true selves. Passively yielding seems so much easier, but it makes us resentful and angry. Fortunately, we can move from unhealthy passivity to gracious assertiveness. In my experience, this happens in three phases.

1. *Request.* Our first step in breaking out of the trap of passivity is to ask for what we need. James said, "You do not have because you do not ask" (James 4:2). Many of us expect our needs to be met but never actually ask. Some wives fall into the pattern of trying to collect on their expectations from their spouses by resorting to nagging and constant criticism. Typically, husbands respond by building higher walls, which in turn triggers greater attempts on the wives' part to penetrate the walls and this leads husbands to fortify the walls even more.

Suggest to those same women that they simply ask for what they need, and they react in shock, stating, "He should know what I need!" Well, he should, but he may not. Or he may be denying it or seeing how far he can push you. These women have a choice. They can ask and possibly get what they need, or they can refuse to ask and never get it. Asking doesn't guarantee one's needs will be met, but it does open up possibilities.

Use the formula of fact, feeling, and follow-through: (1) state the fact, (2) express your feeling, and (3) ask for follow-through. Here is an example: "You withdraw into the sports channel every night after dinner. I feel lonely and neglected. Could we do the dishes together and spend fifteen minutes talking?" Demands create a power struggle, whereas asking elicits the will and sometimes draws out a very positive, even heroic, response.

2. *Appeal.* If asking fails, the next step in assertiveness is to appeal to the conscience. Confronting wrong

in another person is sometimes necessary, even for wrong done to us. We are told, "Admonish one another" (Romans 15:14). Explain that the current situation has been hurtful. An important key in this process is found in Paul's counsel: "Do not rebuke an older man, but exhort him as a father, younger men as brothers, older women as mothers, younger women as sisters, with all purity" (1 Timothy 5:1, 2). Avoid judgmental rebuking but rather *exhort,* which in the Greek *parakalei* means "call to one's side," calling them to the standard of their own principles. Telling someone, "Hey, you are better than this!" often yields results, while telling the person, "You are a failure," well, *fails.*

Don't let the appeal step turn into a lifestyle of guilt mongering and complaining. If changes don't come, it may be time to take the next step.

3. *Demand.* When all else fails, it may be necessary to issue an ultimatum—a demand that our rights and needs be respected. Demands involve consequences, so make sure you identify the consequences ahead of time. Often they will simply be the discontinuation of accommodating and enabling behaviors the abuser has come to expect. Sometimes they will involve serious logistical or legal steps, such as separation or divorce. Think carefully about what consequences would fit the wrong, and tell your loved one plainly what those consequences will be.

Remember, you can't choose for others, but you can choose for yourself. You can't tell others what to do, but you can tell them what you will do in response to what they do. A friend whose philandering husband had carried on for years with another woman finally served him with divorce papers. A great cheer went up from those who knew of her enabling, and the bold move ultimately shocked him into reality and he ended his illicit relationship.

Not all women lack assertiveness, but it is a learned skill for many of us. Some of us cycle wildly between stuffing our feelings and exploding in rage, earning ourselves unpleasant reputations. Counterintuitively, the cure for aggression is not passivity but gracious assertiveness that respects ourselves and others. Women need not sit quietly, costing nothing, leaving only tiptoe footprints in the world. We can stand up and be counted. When we do, marvelous things can happen.

One day I received a call from an important church administrator, inviting me to speak for a pastors' retreat. Me? A woman in lay ministry, speak for pastors? I jumped at what I thought was a great opportunity, forgetting to discuss the sticky issue of finances. Being a self-employed lay minister, I must negotiate my paycheck with every engagement, and sometimes I end up forgetting or avoiding this awkward task.

I preached my heart out at the retreat, delivering my last sermon on Mary Magdalene with an emphasis on pouring out our lives in service. Suddenly, it occurred to me that I was doing just that—pouring myself out for no earthly compensation. I had totally forgotten to negotiate the speaker's fee.

God and the angels must have been holding their stomachs in laughter when the hosting group then presented me with the customary thank-you gift bag. Typically, the bag contains soaps, lotions, bath salts, and a crisp little envelope holding some kind of honorarium.

This time? They gave me gooseberry pancake mix. And that's all.

I thanked them profusely and let it go. After all, I was the one who forgot to be assertive, and they didn't owe me anything. But something else happened that weekend—something priceless. I met a kind pastor who had published some popular books on prayer. In the middle of one of our chats, he asked, "Jennifer, have you ever been anointed for ministry?"

"Not formally by human beings. I hope I have been anointed by God."

"Would you be willing for my wife and me to hold a special anointing service for you?"

I saw God's hand. That day He looked down at me holding my gooseberry pancake mix and said, "You know, this girl needs to be anointed."

"The refining, softening influence of Christian women is needed in the great work of preaching the truth. The Lord of the vineyard is saying to many women who are now doing nothing, 'Why stand ye here all day idle?' Zealous and continued diligence in our sisters toiling for the spread of the truth would be wholly successful, and would astonish us with its results. Through patience and perseverance, the work must be accomplished."[3]

Why stand idle? God sees astonishing potential in you. Look up, stand up, and speak up.

Journaling

What are some areas in your life where you could use more assertiveness, and what actions can you take toward that?

_____

_____

_____

_____

_____

_____

_____

_____

_____

_____

Prayer

Dear gracious Assertiveness-Training Coach,

I have been passive, aggressive, and passive-aggressive at times when I should have been graciously assertive. I hate displeasing people, so I appease them. But then I feel taken advantage of, and I lash out at them, myself, or both. I am done with this! Teach me, Coach, how to assert myself graciously so that I can practice respect for everyone involved. Amen.

1. David Sack, " 'Addicted' to an Addict? 5 Warning Signs of Codependency," *Addiction Recovery* (blog), Psych Central, accessed December 3, 2017, https://blogs .psychcentral.com/addiction-recovery/2012/09/5-warning-signs-codependency/.

2. In the United States, call 1-800-799-7233 (1-800-799-SAFE) for the National Domestic Abuse Hotline. The Hot Peach Pages organization has a website (http://www.hotpeachpages.net/) with an international directory of domestic violence agencies.

3. Ellen G. White, "Address and Appeal, Setting Forth the Importance of Missionary Work," *Review and Herald*, January 2, 1879, 1.

Chapter 13

Daughterling

Jesus Calls You. Arise!

Many of Jesus' noteworthy exchanges were with women. In the Gospel of Mark, we find one of the most "womeny" stories of all.

Imagine the scene. Jesus has just crossed the Sea of Galilee, where He cast demons into a herd of swine. The sun beats down on a crowd gathered by the shore. A man steps forth, a ruler of the synagogue, and throws himself at Jesus' feet, crying, "My little daughter lies at the point of death. Come and lay Your hands on her, that she may be healed, and she will live" (Mark 5:23).

The synagogue rulers lord it over the little people and never ask help from anyone. But this mighty religious leader comes down from his lofty perch, driven by a fear so embedded in his heart that it bypasses the anxiety of humiliation. Life has finally dealt him a blow that cracks him wide open, and he cares not if he loses his status, his standing, or his job. His term "my little daughter" is *thugatrion*, literally "daughterling." Just imagine him: powerful, strong, dignified, but crumbling, broken, weeping, choking out, "My daughterling . . . [sob] is dying [gasp]. Please, Jesus, touch her and save her!"

Of course, Jesus responds to this prayer, turning His feet toward the girl's sickbed.

But when one walks with a Divine Healer, one must suffer through the short stops—a lost child here, a hungry beggar there, a guilt-ridden adulteress, a paralytic, a demoniac— you know, a typical stroll through town with Jesus. Among Jesus' distractions is a poor woman who has been trying to press through the crowd for some time. She finally finds herself within a few feet of Him. This woman has menstruated continually for twelve years; the lifeblood continuously draining out of her. Money means nothing to the sick, and she has spent all of hers on procedures and medicines that have failed to stanch the flow.

"If I can but touch His garment," she murmurs, summoning up every iota of vital force to press her withering hand toward Him. There! She barely touches the edge of His robe. Before she can fully feel the disease-healing vigor now coursing through her body, He wheels around, questioning, "Who touched Me?" (verse 31).

Shy and humble, she finds concealment impossible, so she casts herself at His feet. In the purest, most overflowing love, the Life-Giver says, "Daughter, your faith has made you well. Go in peace, and be healed of your affliction" (verse 34). For the first time in what feels like an eon, she rises in strength.

Abruptly, a messenger brings the news that the ruler's *daughterling* is dead.

That dry ache in the pit of the stomach. That hopeless sorrow that melts a strong man to shaking tears. That sense of loss before life was ever fully gained. *She was only twelve. And now she's gone. Oh, my daughterling.*

Then the scene shifts again when Jesus' voice calls the father's hope from the pit just as it will soon call the daughter from the grave. "Do not be afraid; only believe," He says (verse 36).

The two press on to the home, which is now circled by hired mourners and noisy flutists. Wading through the crowd, Jesus utters a strange announcement: "Why make this commotion and weep? The child is not dead, but sleeping" (verse 39).

But we saw her die! We know death—that pallor, that ebbing away of color, that final collapse of the nerves, the smell. This guy is crazy!

Laughter. Scorn.

She's just sleeping. Ha.

Never mind the mocking. Jesus shuts all but the immediate family and His three disciples out of the house, walks to the bedside of the sleeping *thugatrion*, and intones, "Talitha, cumi" (verse 41). "Damsel, arise!"

Every dimension of the universe, from subatomic particles to galaxies in space, shift their death-accommodating position to obey the will of their Commander. Life flows into the space left by evicted death, filling the girl's limp body, electrifying every cell. She immediately rises to her feet, dancing around the room like any twelve-year-old. Daddy folds her into his massive arms. *You are alive! You are alive! I love you, Talitha, my* thugatrion. The home becomes a scene of otherworldly ebullience as waves of awe, relief, and joy wash over the loved ones. Heaven has touched Earth, and Earth can't help but party.

And so in the space of a few hours, Jesus heals two women: one old, one young; one sick, one dead. Each and every one of us is represented in one of those women, and in these stories, we see our hope: The Life-Giver lives to give us life—His life.

We have journeyed through the story of womankind, witnessing her creation, her fall, and her rising again in the Redeemer's love. We have seen how the enemy of womankind has exploited sin's consequences to make our suffering much more than God ever intended. We have also seen how God can mightily use us even in the midst of that suffering.

We have seen how our own bad choices can increase the suffering, and we have learned how to make healthier and holier ones to honor the One who died for us. We have come to the last chapter of the journey, to the thundering command of the Lover and Life-Giver of women, "Damsel, arise!" He says to us today, *Get up! Get up! Get off your bed. Come forth from your grave. I have raised you to infinite potential in Me. Rise up, my daughterling. I am waiting to dance around the room with you.*

Journaling

Why do you love Jesus? What would you do if you found yourself in His physical presence?

_____

_____

_____

_____

_____

_____

_____

_____

_____

_____

_____

Prayer

Dear resurrected King,

Thank You for calling me from death to life. I want to arise; I *will* arise because You have called me. I choose life because You, Life itself, have given me this gift. I have never known anyone like You with Your infinite, unfailing, and unfathomable love. Thank You for calling me forth. Thank You, my King and my God! Amen.

Notes